ONE FRIDAY IN APRIL

The Emerald Light in the Air: Stories

The Afterlife: A Memoir

The Verificationist: A Novel

The Hundred Brothers: A Novel

Elect Mr. Robinson for a Better World: A Novel

ONE FRIDAY IN APRIL

A Story of Suicide and Survival

DONALD ANTRIM

W. W. NORTON & COMPANY
Independent Publishers Since 1923

For information about permission to reproduce selections from this book, write to Permissions, W. W. Norton & Company, Inc., 500 Fifth Avenue, New York, NY 10110

For information about special discounts for bulk purchases, please contact W. W. Norton Special Sales at specialsales@wwnorton.com or 800-233-4830

Manufacturing by Lakeside Book Company
Book design by Chris Welch
Production manager: Lauren Abbate

Library of Congress Cataloging-in-Publication Data

Names: Antrim, Donald, author.
Title: One Friday in April : a story of suicide and survival /
Donald Antrim.
Description: First edition. | New York, NY : W. W. Norton & Company,
[2021] | Includes bibliographical references.
Identifiers: LCCN 2021022098 | ISBN 9781324005568 (hardcover) |
ISBN 9781324005575 (epub)
Subjects: LCSH: Antrim, Donald—Mental health. | Authors, American—
Biography. | Suicide—United States.
Classification: LCC HV6545 .A68 2021 | DDC 362.28/092 [B]—dc23
LC record available at https://lccn.loc.gov/2021022098

W. W. Norton & Company, Inc.
500 Fifth Avenue, New York, N.Y. 10110
www.wwnorton.com

W. W. Norton & Company Ltd.
15 Carlisle Street, London W1D 3BS

1 2 3 4 5 6 7 8 9 0

For Marija

Ask not what disease the person has, but rather,
what person the disease has.

—SIR WILLIAM OSLER

ONE FRIDAY IN APRIL

ONE FRIDAY IN APRIL 2006, I SPENT THE AFTERNOON AND evening pacing the roof of my apartment building in Brooklyn, climbing down the fire-escape ladder and hanging by my hands from the railing, then climbing back up with sore palms and lying on the roof, in a ball, or stretched out on my back or on my stomach, maybe peering surreptitiously over the roof ledge. The roof is painted silver. The building is four stories tall. A group of my friends, each of whom had been on the phone with me, one after the other, all through the morning, when I'd been alone and dialing wildly, had got busy calling each other. Janice owned a car, and she and Nicky were coming across the bridge from Manhattan, but there was traffic, and no one knew where I was.

From the roof, the world seemed to scream. I heard sirens—police, ambulance, and fire. What agency would come for me? A helicopter was flying overhead and circling back. The woman I'd just run from, the woman who had rushed over ahead of the others, who had been with me downstairs in my apartment, my partner then, Regan, thought that I'd gone to the street. We had been fighting over something I'd done. I'd hurt her, and we were both in anguish. She spoke harshly, and I ran away to die and end her burden. She charged after me, but the wrong way, down instead of up, out the front door of the building and toward the avenue. The sun was setting, and the sky over New Jersey was orange, and I was in my socks, shivering. I was afraid for my life. I didn't know why I had to fall from the roof, why that was mine to do.

When telling the story of my illness, I try not to speak about depression. I prefer to call it suicide. The American novelist William Styron, in his memoir *Darkness Visible: A Memoir of Madness*, argues that the word "depression" is inadequate to describe this illness, and I agree. A depression is a concavity, a sloping downward and a return. Suicide, in my experience, is not that. I believe that suicide is a natural history, a disease process, not an act or a choice, a decision or a wish. I do not understand suicide as a response to pain, or as a message to the living—or not only as those things. I do not think of suicide as the act, the death, the fall from a height or the trigger pulled. I see it as a long illness, an illness with origins in trauma and isolation, in deprivation of touch, in violence and neglect, in the loss of home and belonging. It is a disease of the body and the brain, if you make that distinction, but its etiology, its beginning, whether in early or later life, in the family or beyond, is social in nature. I see suicide as a social disease. I will refer to suicide, not depression.

My sickness lasted years. It continued after that Friday on the roof, and went on for more than a decade, through long hospitalizations and more than fifty rounds of electroconvulsive therapy, once known as shock therapy. It lasted through a decade of recovery, relapse, and recovery. Those times seem far removed, though they can also feel recent in memory. Up on the roof, I felt as if I had been dying all my life. I felt that it had begun when I was a little child.

I was hanging from the fire escape. I kept a toehold. The sun was low; the air was cold. I was wearing socks but no shoes, and my palms were scraped and beginning to blister from my letting go a little, one hand at a time, falling out at an angle, sideways or backward, then grabbing fast for the rail, and clutching tight. I gazed down at the concrete patio and the chain-link fence surrounding the backyard. The yard was inaccessible, small, and neglected. My apartment is on the third floor, and windows in my kitchen and bedroom overlook it, though you'd have to stick your head out to see much. I'd never looked at the yard for more than a minute, or heard anyone in it.

Below me was the small patio area littered with trash, and an outdoor stairwell leading to the locked basement and the boiler. The rest was hard ground. Since that time, since 2006, new people, a family, have moved into the first-floor apartment, and they've replaced the old chain-link fence with one made of wood and put in a barbecue and a picnic table; I can hear their children when it's warm out, along with, on school days, even in the cold winter months, older children, neighborhood kids, playing and screaming on the rooftop playground of the private school a few doors down the street.

Recess was over; school was out; night was falling. I had no children. I held on to the railing. It was less dizzying to look down than up. Clouds blew across the sky. Here and there, I could see people having after-work cocktails on private decks on neighboring roofs—it was the beginning of a spring weekend. Now, remembering that day, I wonder what those people might have thought of the man scrambling from fire escape to rooftop and back, letting go with one hand, flopping down on his belly to crane over the edge. Did they imagine that he was doing work, maintenance or repair, some job they couldn't clearly make out? If they had known the man's troubles, had known the man, would they have understood that he was about to die? Or would they have imagined that he was trying to live?

It was getting darker, and I could hear traffic on the street below, people driving home through Brooklyn after work. I was cold; I'd been up there a long time. I didn't know that it had been five hours. It could have been any amount of time. I had on pants, a shirt, and socks. My hands and clothes were dirty from the rooftop. My pants fit loosely, and were falling down. I'd become thin over the winter. Where was my belt? I shoved my hands in my pockets and squeezed my arms to my sides, trying to get warm.

I'd written about my mother, her alcoholic life and her resignation in death, and my role as her son, savior, and abandoner. I began writing the year after she died, too soon for writing to be safe. The book was an accounting of the death of my family. Writing the book had been an excitement, but publishing was an ordeal. The book was a movement from exposition to scene, defense to acceptance, mortification to love. But my old worlds—Charlottesville, Gainesville, Miami, Sarasota;

all the places of my childhood—were costly to rebuild. I worked at betrayal, mine of my mother, hers of me, mine of myself.

I was born in Sarasota, Florida, on a September night in 1958. In the story that my mother tells of my birth, I was taken from her by force. Her mother, my grandmother, pulled me out of my mother's arms and kept me. My mother was not allowed to hold me. My father, who had graduated from college the summer before on an ROTC scholarship, was away, training to command tanks at Fort Bragg, North Carolina, where, eleven months later, my sister, Terry, would be born. My mother told me that she and I were distraught; I cried and cried, but her mother would not give me back. There was panic, she told me, and more fighting and crying, and it took my father a day and a night to get there.

Where was my grandfather? I knew my mother's father as a docile, suffering man. When I was very little, he'd fallen off the roof of the house, while replacing tiles, and broken his back. The house was a two-story white stucco bungalow with a red tile roof, venetian blinds in the windows, a mowed lawn, a paved driveway and carport, a front door that wasn't used, a guest bedroom downstairs, and three bedrooms upstairs. My sister and I lived with our grandparents when our parents were divorcing for the first time. Terry was five and I was six.

We lay awake in separate bedrooms, in the heat. Fans blew. Downstairs, a sun porch with orchids and potted shrubs faced a little square yard planted with orange and tangerine trees. There was wisteria and hibiscus. The air was wet and sticky. Down a little walkway out back was the two-story garage where my grandfather spent part of each day, where he had tools hung on a pegboard, stacked paint cans, a worktable with a vise, and beer in an old refrigerator. The garage smelled of paint thinner, insecticide, and lawnmower gas. My grandfather sat at a bench and mended kitchen-cabinet drawers, or rewired appliances, or sanded wood, while sipping from a can. He chewed cinnamon chewing gum and toothpicks.

My mother was subjected to Munchausen syndrome by proxy—also known as factitious disorder imposed on another—a form of abuse that is carried out, usually by a parent or caregiver, as medical or surgical intervention. My mother recounted a succession of unnecessary operations, heart operations, demanded by her mother and performed by compliant doctors. In one story she told, she was a teenager, at Sarasota Memorial Hospital. Under anesthesia on the operating table, her chest cut open, she heard the doctors pronounce her dead. She could not move or speak, but she could see them peering down at her. The long story of forced visits to doctors, of my grandmother's control of her daughter's body, the authoritarian cycle of manipulation, intimate violation, and symbolic repair, was never understood in my family, and it implicates my grandmother and my grandfather, together in collusion or complicity, in crimes against their only child. "They drank," my mother told me shortly before she died. She told me that her parents fought and were violent toward each other, and that her mother had tried to drown her in a well when she was a baby. She told me that my grandfather was not her real father, and that no one knew the truth about anything.

I was in my socks on the fire escape. I was cold, underweight, and scratched up from the roof's rough surface, from crawling to the edge and leaning over to peer down. I imagined my body on the ground. It was something that I could picture. But the fall, how long would that last? Might I, during the seconds of falling, regret my own death? Would dying hurt? I'd had no intention of running to the roof. I'd run up the stairs without deciding, and I'd climbed onto the fire escape without deciding. The idea of letting go was terrifying. I did it again and again, though. It would have been easy to miss catching the railing. My motor control was failing. I held the railing, then let go a little, and then grabbed hold, and then let go again, but caught myself.

I was not on the roof to jump. I was there to die, but dying was not a plan. I was not making choices, threats, or mistakes. Is this what we mean by impulsive behavior? I was, I think, looking back now, in acceptance. It was a relinquishing, though at the time I would not have been able to articulate that. I did not want to die, only felt that I would, or should, or must, and I had my pain and my reasons, my certainties. If you have had this illness, then you've had your reasons; and maybe you've believed, or still believe, as I have, that it would be better for others, for all the people who have made the mistake of loving you, or who one day might, if you were gone.

Depression, hysteria, melancholia, nervousness, neurosis, neurasthenia, madness, lunacy, insanity, delirium, derangement, demonic possession, black humors, black bile, the blues, the blue devil, a brown study, a broken heart, a funk, a storm, a brainstorm, the abyss, an inferno, an apocalypse, Hell, the Void, anxiety, a lack of affect, panic, loneliness, bad wiring, irritability, hostility, unipolar disorder, bipolar disorder, mixed depression, post-traumatic stress disorder, obsessive-compulsive disorder, attention-deficit disorder, borderline personality disorder, bulimia, anorexia, rumination, grief, mourning, malingering, laziness, sadness, despondency, dysfunction, dysthymia, detachment, disassociation, dementia praecox, neuralgia, oversensitivity, hypersensitivity, idiocy, unreasonableness, an unsound mind, cowardice, obstinacy, obduracy, intransigence, instability, apathy, lethargy, ennui, recalcitrance, battle fatigue, shell shock, self-pity, self-indulgence, weakness, withdrawal, delusion, dissatisfaction, negativity, a turn in the barrel, a break in a life narrative, bad thoughts, bad feelings, falling apart, falling to pieces, wigging out, freaking out, a chemical imbalance, a heavy heart, self-destructiveness, excitation, exhaustion, thoughts of hurting oneself or others, the thousand-yard stare, rage, misery, gloom, desolation, wretchedness, hopelessness, unworthiness, mania, morbidity, genius, terror, dread, a descent, a fall, suicidality, suicidal ideation, aggression, regression, deregulation, decompensation, deadness, drama, agony, angst, breakdown, a disease of the mind, a disorder, heartbreak, rough sailing, crackup, catatonia, agitation, losing one's mind, losing one's way, losing heart, wasting away, a crisis, a struggle, a trial, existential despair, a philosophical problem, a decision taken after long thought, shame, shyness, ranting and raving, the furies, an old friend, a constant companion, a punishment, a tragedy, a curse, a crime against nature, a crime against God, a sin, a mystery, an enigma, and, of course, psychosis—suicide, in the past and in our own time, has been called, and attributed to, many things.

I was thin and cold. I held my arms to my sides. I peered up at the clouds and the jet planes and the sunset. It was hard to look at the sky. I couldn't hold my head up. I was taking a benzodiazepine, Klonopin, for anxiety and insomnia. My mother was dead, and my socks had holes. The light hurt my eyes, and sounds felt like sharp little jabs at my head; when the helicopter came, that afternoon on the roof, I hunched over, protectively, as if I were being hit. Was the helicopter coming for me? Regan had raised her voice with me.

She and I were in the living room. This wasn't our first close relationship. We'd got together in 1994, and stayed together until 1999. But we had a tough time. We were combative with each other, and our arguments reminded me of my parents' nightly battles. Right before we met, she lost her mother, and was for a long time in grief. We broke up and got back together more than once. We never lived together, but we lived near each other.

Regan and I had been together—the second time around—for only a few months, since the summer of 2005. That Friday in April, she rushed to Brooklyn from her office in Manhattan, panicked after hearing my voice on the phone; and of course Janice and Nicky were on their way in Janice's car, in traffic. Regan had stayed with me, done her best to help me. She was sleep-deprived, anxious, angry, afraid, untouched, breathing my cigarette smoke, not eating, not laughing, morose—the winter. Then, in early spring, I had staggered into Manhattan and spent the night with a former girlfriend.

Regan screamed at me that I would go to Hell, and that she hoped I would die.

I wrote so many notes. Most suicides don't; we don't leave testaments. I wrote them all winter long, on a notepad, while sitting on a tarp on the living room floor. Writing, moving my arm, my wrist, my hand, was effortful. My grip on the pen was rigid, and my hands ached, and were always cold. I wrote an opening, tore the page from the pad, and began another note. The notes were apologies. Sometimes I called friends and held them on the phone. I was fine, I told them. When I lay down, I crossed my arms over my chest, in the position of a corpse.

But then I was up, startled, pacing, shaking, scared, awake without having slept, worrying about my heart, spreading out the tarp, not wanting to leave a mess, and then sitting with pills, pad, pen, and a knife, an old Sabatier that had been in our kitchen when I was a boy. The blade was rusty. None of the letters got finished. My heart pounded. I knelt on the living room floor and forced myself to cough as hard as I could, coughing and coughing, on my hands and knees, spitting up on the carpet. Maybe I could induce a heart attack. One day, the zipper on my winter coat jammed, and the metal zipper handle broke off, and I felt that my life was coming to an end. I drew the blade of the knife across my wrist. How much pressure would it take to cut through the skin?

Would I be better off bleeding in warm water in the tub? I was frantic, worn out but unable to stay still. At the end of each day, at around five or five-thirty, before Regan came over after work, I stowed the tarp, replaced the knife in the kitchen drawer, cleaned the ashtray, put away the pills, and buried the suicide notes in the garbage.

On the roof, late that day in April, after running from the apartment and up the stairs, after hanging from the fire escape, letting go in stages, I climbed the ladder to the roof and huddled against the stairwell bulkhead, next to the door to the stairs. I was breathing fast, and my body hurt. Night was falling. Beyond the Brooklyn rooftops was Manhattan. Lights were on in the skyscrapers. The pain seemed to come from my skin and my muscles and my joints and my bones. But when I touched myself, I couldn't find a source. I felt like I hurt everywhere, but also nowhere. My chest was constricted, as if a weight were pressing in—but from where? There was no weight, no feeling of a source or origin or cause, nothing to palpate. I'd say that it was the pain of being crushed or squeezed to death, but I've never been crushed or squeezed to death. Have you? Have you felt as if your body were collapsing from the inside, collapsing and hardening? Where was Regan? Where were my friends? I wanted a bullet. I'd wanted one since Christmas, to eliminate an itch behind my temple. I imagined the bullet easing in. Was Jesus waiting, or a trip into brightness, some stellar afterlife? Was death knowledge, or might I wake up, a baby again, born into some new violence? What were the chances? Might I, after falling, be alive but maimed? And if I were gone, might Regan live?

I grew up sleep-deprived. I was always sick. I couldn't keep up in school, and often missed days. I had anxiety, allergies, and asthma; and irritable bowel, and headaches, and, starting in fifth grade, when I was ten, awful and incapacitating back spasms. They began early one morning before school, in the upstairs bathroom in our house on Lewis Mountain Road in Charlottesville, while I was bending over the toilet, throwing up after a night of staring around my dark bedroom, struggling to breathe, listening to the fighting.

Sometimes in the middle of the night, my sister and I crept out of our rooms and sat in our pajamas on the landing, behind the banister, afraid to look. You could say of our childhood that she played in her room, while I went out in the yard. Or you could say that she fled into her room, and that I fled outside. I made friends, but my friends were always changing; our family moved almost yearly, moved up and down the southern Atlantic seaboard, or sometimes just across town—Sarasota, Gainesville, Charlottesville, Tallahassee, back again to Charlottesville, and then south again, down Interstate 95 to Miami. Pretty much every year, we moved to a new house; single-story, two-story; driveways, sidewalks; screened porch, no porch; three cats, four cats; swimming pools, beaches, ponds; a converted army barracks in Gainesville, Florida; a bungalow in Tallahassee; an apartment and then a two-story house in Charlottesville, Virginia; suburban tract houses in Miami; a farm at the foot of the Blue Ridge.

I remember, as best I can, the houses. I remember the crying, and the thuds on the floor in the next room. If our father kills our mother, and the judge asks me what I saw, what will I say? If our mother kills our father, and the judge orders me to tell, how can I speak? If our father goes to prison, what will happen to Terry and me? If our mother goes to prison, what will we do? How can I prosecute my father? How can I accuse my mother?

I imagined myself on the witness stand. I was in fifth grade. I was failing math. For a time, I had tutoring, but still couldn't solve the problems. The tutor was a friend of my mother's. She talked, and I imagined a courthouse. There was a lawyer, and it was quiet; people waited for me to speak.

There were knives in the kitchen. I remember a night in Charlottesville, when I was ten and Terry nine, the year in the house on Lewis Mountain Road. I heard my mother scream that my father had a knife and was trying to kill her. My father was a young professor, a T. S. Eliot man, at the university. I don't have good memories of him, only memories. But even the bad memories somehow don't include him, though he was right there, hung over, maudlin, a phantom. He died in 2009, of a heart attack, after falling asleep on my stepmother's shoulder, on a layover in their journey from Fort Worth to Venice for Christmas. He was seventy-three. Maybe the knife that my mother was screaming about that night was the Sabatier that I took from the drawer when I left home, back in the mid-1970s or so, and then, nearly thirty years later, carried from my own kitchen in Brooklyn, through the bedroom, up the hall, past the bathroom and the office that I didn't use, moving fast, off-balance and stumbling to the living room, where I laid it on the plastic tarp, beside the pills, and then sat on the tarp, next to the pills and the knife, waiting out the day, not yet dead.

When I was a boy, I brought the covers up to my chin, wrapped them tightly around me, and lay without moving in bed. I held my arms close to my sides, or crossed over my chest. I gazed up at my model airplanes, moonlit, hanging from threads from the ceiling. My chest, my body, felt tight, tight in the sense of a contraction, but also tight in the sense of being bound and squeezed. I felt paralyzed, or not exactly that, though something like that. I wasn't paralyzed. Was I paralyzed? It was safest to lie still. Nonetheless, I shook, though not in a way that you'd notice—it was more of a hum. I felt numb yet in pain, and breathed shallow breaths, restrained.

Even now, in my sixties, if I cry hard, I will be frightened, and you may find me in a corner, crouched, and turned toward the wall, my hands raised to protect my face. I will sob and shake, and make myself small, and beg, *Please, go away.* I will not be able to look at you. If you touch me, I will scream in pain and run from the room. Why can't you see that it would be better for you without me? If any one feeling has defined my life, it is the feeling, more an awareness than a thought, that only lonely rooms are safe. This is how I feel and imagine shame, not as guilt or regret or remorse, not as some particular emotion or amalgam of emotions, but as a basic provision, abjection, the condition of those who have been neglected, harmed, cast out.

The sun was down, and I was on the roof. I couldn't stand straight. I couldn't walk straight. I couldn't pull my shoulders back, or take a deep breath. I was forty-seven, middle-aged, in the time of life when, for men living on their own, the incidence of suicide rises. I could see the city in all directions. The summer before, the summer of 2005, I'd finished and handed in my book about my mother. It was scheduled to come out in July. My friends Janice and Nicky had driven from Manhattan across the

East River, and Regan had run out of the apartment to the street. That had been earlier, it seemed to me, such a long time before. There had been a plane in the sky. There'd been that helicopter. I realized that I would go to a hospital. I'd been ruminating over hospitals, imagining them, fearing them. The doctors would drug and shock me. Best to stay away from hospitals. On the roof, looking over the city, I pictured gothic piles and state psychiatric prisons, stone dungeons and brick barracks; and the wards, paint peeling, floors stained, locked and dark, fenced in.

I opened the door to the stairs, stepped through, and locked the bolt behind me. For months, Regan and others had told me that I wasn't well, that I needed to get better. What did they mean, better? When had I been better—when had that been? I imagined that I would be in the hospital, in hospitals, for a long time. I'd been seeing my then psychotherapist, M—my third since moving to New York in 1983—on the Upper East Side, as well as, for prescriptions, a psychiatrist connected to a Brooklyn hospital. Sometime around the New Year, my heart started pounding. I checked my pulse over and over with a watch, hour after hour, day after day. Regan assured me that my heart was normal, but I contradicted her, and then asked for reassurance. I paced, and every night at two, three, four o'clock, woke up in fear. Waking was sudden—the new dark day. My gut seized, and I rolled into a ball. I felt as if my body were burning. I wasn't suicidal, was I? I was only jagged and tired, and my heart beat too rapidly. What a ruthless act, writing about my mother. But I had the comforting thought that at least I wasn't suicidal. I wouldn't do anything to myself. I would never do that. Looking back, I see that my apprehension of suicide first came as a denial of it. I'd tried antidepressants, years before, unsuccessfully, and again, also unsuccessfully, during the months leading up to the day on the roof: SSRIs, which target the mechanisms that control the neurotransmitter serotonin; an NSRI, affecting serotonin and norepinephrine; Wellbutrin, a dopamine enhancer; and Lamictal, a mood stabilizer developed to treat seizures, now also used to treat a range of clinical conditions. Klonopin is a strongly sedating drug with a long half-life. Like other drugs in the benzodiazepine family, Valium, Ativan, and so on, it is addictive. Over time I adapted to a schedule, one little yellow pill, four times per day, a schedule around which, over the winter and into the spring, I organized my worsening days and nights, counting down the hours and minutes to each new pill.

I recall a visit to the psychiatrist in his office. It was March, not long before I ran to the roof. Leaving the house for any reason was scary and difficult; I felt, walking out of the building and down the sidewalk, as if I could not make it to the corner, and often I didn't. My legs were heavy, and trembled; out on the street, the pain in my chest became sharper and more crushing. I told the doctor that I thought that the Klonopin might be making things worse.

He was sitting at his desk. He sketched a picture on a piece of paper. It was a picture of crossing perpendicular lines with a waveform running along the horizontal axis, a graph showing a sine curve. The sections of the curve below the axis he labeled "Depression," and the area above the axis "Anxiety." The doctor explained that benzodiazepines might worsen depression but help with anxiety, and that I seemed to have more anxiety than depression, and that there should be a middle ground. He pointed to the picture. It was an explanation for a child. He was trying to reach me, as we say, to get through to me. Why couldn't I understand? His voice was insistent, and I could hear, and feel, that he wanted the session to end. Agony and anxiety. I told the doctor that I understood the drawing, but nonetheless believed that the medication was its own problem. He wanted me to try cognitive behavioral therapy, which focuses directly on symptoms, thoughts, and behaviors, rather than on the origins and historical experience of illness in the patient's life. The doctor asked if I had been thinking of hurting myself. Was I having suicidal thoughts?

I made it down the first flight from the roof, and then the second. My clothes were filthy, and my hands were black. I held the banister. I wasn't going to die that day. I padded in torn socks along the landing to my apartment. The door was unlocked. Regan, Nicky, and Janice were in the living room. Janice and Nicky didn't know each other. Or had they already met? Who told Janice to pick up Nicky and drive to Brooklyn? My friends had reacted to the sound of my voice, that morning when I'd called person after person, called and called, and then run from the apartment to the roof. When I came back down the stairs, I knew only that they were there. They backed away at first. Where had I gone? Why had I run away and scared them?

They stood in a circle around me. Nicky told me that we were leaving for the hospital. The psychiatrist had arranged for a room. I told my friends that I wanted a cigarette. My face was dirty, and I must've looked wild. Nicky told me to forget the cigarette. I put on my glasses. I put on a belt and a coat, and then we all went downstairs, got in Janice's car, and drove to the wrong hospital. We ran into the emergency room, got directions to the right hospital, and ran back to the car. You would've thought that I was dying. I watched the traffic and the lights.

We were there. Regan helped with the forms, and later Janice and Nicky drove back to Manhattan. A nurse came with a plastic bag, and I took off my belt and unlaced my shoes and tugged the laces through their holes and handed them over, and Regan and I put laces, keys, change, and the belt, anything that might be used for harm, in the bag. The nurse took the bag, and I was led to a small room. Regan waited with me.

A doctor came. The doctor asked how I was feeling. I named the wrongs I'd done in my life, the people I'd hurt, catastrophes and losses. He told me to try not to worry about all that—I needed to get well. I asked him why he didn't hear what I was saying, and he told me that when I felt better I might take a different view of my life. I asked him how long I would be in the hospital, and he said that he didn't know. Then Regan had to go. It was late at night. I told her that I didn't want her to leave me. After a while, a man arrived with a wheelchair. He rolled me through the halls to the elevator. Upstairs, on the ward, I told the nurse that I'd been taking Klonopin, but thought that it was having a bad effect, and asked for Ativan, a shorter-acting benzodiazepine, and she saw her way to that, and I woke up the next morning in a white room with a narrow view of rooftops.

I was in a room of my own. There wasn't much to it. The ward was rectangular, with a nursing station and medication dispensary, an isolation room for stressed or threatening patients, and, behind the scenes, offices, supply cabinets, closets, restrooms, and, presumably, a communal area for the staff. Patients' bedrooms lined the hallways. A common area doubled as the dining room. The television was on all day. Patients leaned in doorways and sat on beds. Nurses checked the rooms, counting us every twenty minutes throughout the day and night. Many of us had had more than one hospitalization. Some knew each other from earlier stays. Had I been admitted before? What was I taking?

By Saturday afternoon, my body felt lighter, and my thoughts, I thought, were pretty clear. Was it the Ativan? I stayed on my bed, or talked on the pay phone down the hall. I called my father and my sister and my friends, and told them where I was, and then joined a table with male patients and a supervisor who gave us disposable razors, shaving cream, and water in cups. My hand shook; the razor scraped my face. I remember a young man who had brain damage from sniffing chemicals from a paper bag. He told me that he was Dominican. He looked like Jesus. He had long black hair, and spoke with kindness, but his sentences ended before communicating much meaning. He passed me a pocket Bible. I still have it. I keep it in a drawer in my bedroom. Regan came during visiting hours. A few old friends were with her that Saturday. Or was it Sunday? The nurse unlocked the door, and my friends showed their backpacks and bags, and signed in, and then we all visited, as my Tennessee relatives used to put it, in the common room. My friends told me that I would get better. What did they know? I wore my own pants and shirt, not a hospital gown. I was ashamed, and they seemed abashed. I felt that. Or I should say that we shared in that.

On Monday, the inpatient doctors and their residents came. The ward busied, like any workplace at the start of a new week. My own doctor, the prescribing doctor, was not at the hospital. I told his colleague that I was all right, and that I believed I could go home.

We were in my room. The doctor was doing morning rounds. I sat on the bed, and she sat on a chair that she'd dragged in from outside. There were no chairs in those rooms. "Do you think you'll be safe?" she asked.

"Yes." I told her that I'd had a scare, but that I didn't think it would happen again.

"How are you feeling now?"

"Much better."

I wasn't lying. I'd slept some.

"Are you having thoughts of harming yourself?"

"No."

"How are you feeling now?"

"I think I'll be OK."

"Can you tell me what brought this on?"

I told the doctor that my mother was an alcoholic

who'd lived a horrible life. I told her about losses and errors of my own, and the doctor watched my face and listened for frequency compression in my voice. Later that day, the hospital approved my discharge. A nurse brought the plastic bag, and I laced my shoes and signed the papers and sorted my things back into my pockets. I put on my coat. The nurse with the keychain led me down the hall and unlocked the door. I left the ward and walked toward the elevators. The door closed behind me, a heavy sound, and then I heard the key in the lock.

I rode the elevator to the lobby. I left the building, crossed the street, and got in a waiting car. Sometimes, when I think of that day, I recall Regan coming to get me, and our going home together. Mainly, though, I remember that I was on my own. It was about three o'clock. I was wobbly. The sun was out, and the sky was blue. I was breathing fast. My skin felt prickly. The world did not look right. Brooklyn was unfamiliar. I don't mean that the driver took a novel route. Was it the brightness in the light, a seeming sharpness to the day, that Monday afternoon? People walked on the sidewalks and crossed at the lights. It was early spring. The houses and shops were in rows, and the trees, a few already flowering, pink, violet, white, stood planted. I recognized Prospect Park, and my neighborhood, and my street. Surely I would be all right. I paid and thanked the driver, and then hurried upstairs, shut the door, and turned the lock. The living room was as I'd left it. Things were where they belonged. The view out the windows hadn't changed. I crumpled onto the sofa. Where was I?

I stayed out of the hospital for five weeks. The symptoms that I'd gone in with, that I'd lived with for months, returned and worsened. I didn't sleep that first night home. Regan told me that I would be all right, it would be all right, but I knew that I wasn't safe. I remember waking, startled, burning with sickness, the sheets and pillows soaked with sweat, the worst kind of waking. I got out of bed and fled up the hall to the front of the apartment, then paced the living room, where I sat down and got up, sat and got up.

It went that way every night, and the same in the daytime, not just most days but every day. The itch in my temple, the need for a bullet, was constant. The itch wasn't topical. It wasn't itchy skin. It lay deep. If I scratched it, if I could somehow dig into my brain and scratch the itch, then I might feel clarity and peace. Without the bullet, I would never have either. But when had I ever felt clear? When had I been peaceful? How long until it was time for another Ativan? Some days, I lay in bed, picturing the bullet moving slowly through my brain. The image soothed me. Outside the window was the fire escape. How to die? Who would find me? Who would have to look back on that scene? I would leave a note, begging Regan not to unlock and open the door, not to come inside the apartment, but to call the police instead. Children played and yelled on the rooftop of the school down the street. My hips and back, my arms and legs felt stiff, though loose, somehow. Later, Regan would come over, and I would try to eat. But my jaw was tight, and it was hard to swallow. I had no appetite. Regan and I spoke less and less. She stayed in the front room, the living room, and I mainly went in back. Sometimes I took out my cell phone and dialed person after person. Or I left long messages.

One day in mid-April, Regan and I took a walk to the Brooklyn Botanic Gardens. I'd been out of the hospital only a short time. It was a Saturday morning. I didn't want to go. How would I make it? How could I escape, if I needed to, from the outdoors? Walking, any movement, seemed too difficult, and I didn't think that I could go far without turning back. The day was bright, and Regan urged me to look up at the blossoming trees. But I couldn't; I couldn't hold my head up. I could not form a smile. I could not tolerate touch. Merely standing was excruciating, and I could only peer at my feet. I felt as if I were immensely heavy. Stumbling through the gardens with Regan, I saw flowers in bloom, and ponds and people, couples and families, but it was exhausting to look. I raised my hands to my forehead, shielding my eyes.

Regan was disappointed, and I was afraid; my chest felt sunken and tight, and I needed to sit, but couldn't bear sitting. I could neither move nor stay still. I did not feel safe in the gardens, or over coffee, or back home. It must have been around this time that I told Regan that this was what rigor mortis might feel like, were one able to experience that in awareness, in life.

What were my crimes? What are yours? What do you look forward to? I looked forward to poverty, abandonment by my remaining family members, the inability to write or work, the dissolution of friendships, professional and artistic oblivion, loneliness and deterioration, institutionalization and the removal from society—abjection and the end of belonging with or among others. I would be alone. The calm that I'd had for a moment in the hospital was gone. I slept two or three hours, and then sat up watching the light change with morning; and, later, during the day, took the death position, phoned those who might answer, or sped from back to front in the apartment, dragging the tarp. It was April, and then May, an eternity in real time. I worried about my shoulders. Over the spring, the joints had seemed to weaken. I could control my arms, but felt also that they were somehow just hanging there. Perhaps this was, as it were, an instance of hypochondria—I'd had a history of dislocations when younger. But what to make of the strange fluctuations in balance when walking, the tipping sideways, one way and then the other; or the effort required to hold a cup or a glass, or write with a pen? How had I become so clumsy and uncoordinated? Why did sounds hurt? Why the adrenaline, the ruminations on death, the bullet and the knife? Were my thoughts of dying intrusive, as we sometimes describe them, or were they simply the only thoughts that I had? When had the light begun to feel like sand thrown in my eyes?

I stumbled downstairs and out of the building. I stuffed keys, cash, and my meds in my pockets, and called a car. The subway was too risky. I would press myself against the platform wall and hyperventilate.

I gave the driver the address, an orthopedic clinic on the Upper East Side, not far from the apartment where I lived in my twenties, back in the time when my mother was getting sober. There's a hospital not far from my apartment in Brooklyn, but it didn't occur to me to go there. On the ride into Manhattan, I lowered the window and felt the air.

When I was a boy, I got carsick. The time that I remember most clearly was in the Smoky Mountains, on hairpin turns outside Asheville, North Carolina. My grandfather was driving, and my grandmother sat beside him, my mother's parents. My sister and I were in the back seat. I must have been seven, going on eight, and Terry six, going on seven. Maybe it was 1965. I looked out the window at trees and valleys, and I could feel the motion of the car. The car was white, with red upholstery, and we were on a trip, and my grandfather liked to speed; and then my grandmother turned and reached back to hand me an apple. It was a yellow apple. The apple was mushy and dry, and the road wound left, right, up, down through the hills. Now, as I write this, I wonder where we were going, where we'd been; and it seems to me that this was a time when our grandparents took my sister and me from our mother and father. We were heading across the mountains, then south to Sarasota, to the house on Wisteria Street. We'd visited Tennessee relatives. Our parents' marriage was ending. I threw up on the seat, and my grandfather stopped the car. He and my grandmother put down towels, and my grandfather told me that if I got sick again I could stick my head out the window and breathe, and I'd feel better.

The clinic was busy. It was a big modern place. I barged up to the desk. The receptionist asked if I had an appointment. I said that I needed a doctor, and she asked me the problem.

"My shoulders."

"Your shoulders?"

People behind the reception desk turned and whispered. I was shaking. I hadn't shaved. I'd got skinnier since my weekend at the hospital, and my clothes were big on me, like clown clothes.

I remember the receptionist telling me that there were no free appointments, but that I could make one for another time. I pleaded, "It's important! Can I talk to a doctor? Isn't there a way?" My throat was tight, and my mouth dry. Did I look decent? Was I shouting?

She told me to wait.

I sat in the waiting room. Was I holding a clipboard, a pen? The waiting room was quiet.

A doctor appeared. He was young, and wore a white coat. Would I please accompany him down the hall?

We went into a room. I didn't climb onto the examination table, and the doctor didn't sit on his rolling stool. We faced each other. He seemed wary. He asked me the problem, and I said, "It's hard to describe. It feels like my arms are falling out of the sockets."

"Both arms?"

I was breathing fast. My heart was beating fast. "It's more on the left."

"Can you rotate?"

I swung my arms in the air. I told the doctor that if I raised and brought my arms too far back the shoulders might dislocate.

He briefly poked and manipulated, going through

the motions, and said, "I'm not finding anything out of the ordinary."

"There is!"

He took a step back and said, "You're welcome to make a regular appointment. But I don't think there's anything wrong with your shoulders."

He told me that he had other patients to see. "Let's go," he said, and then led me back along the hall, past the reception desk, and across the waiting room. People watched. The doctor held the door, and then quietly shut it behind me. I rode the elevator to the lobby. On the street, I called my friend David, who lives in Nyack, twenty miles up the Hudson. David had stayed on the phone with me through the winter and the spring, listening patiently to my jagged talking. I raged to David about my physical condition, and he screamed, "Why aren't you in a hospital? You need to be in a hospital!"

I thought of Anne. We'd been friends in college. She was a year behind me. She'd gone to medical school and become a psychiatrist, and I recalled hearing that she practiced at Columbia Presbyterian, at Broadway and 168th, near the George Washington Bridge and the top of Manhattan. I didn't phone her that day after leaving the clinic, but the next day, or maybe the day after, I got in touch with Anne, and she told me that she was an inpatient doctor, and that she worked in Columbia's psychiatric emergency room.

I was on the little sofa in my living room. I told Anne about the Klonopin and the Ativan, Regan and the roof, the infantilizing doctor and the Brooklyn ward; and I promised her that I was not thinking of hurting myself, though dying was my only thought. I did not need a hospital, I told Anne. What would happen if I told the truth?

She said that I sounded sick. She told me to come to Columbia Presbyterian. They'd take care of me, she said; they'd help me get better. She told me that it was dangerous for me to stay out on my own, that I'd be safe in the hospital, and that I needed treatment. What did she mean, treatment? I told her that I would consider what she was saying. She then gave me the phone number of a colleague in private practice. The colleague's name was Dr. T.

"Everyone respects her," Anne told me.

Dr. T's office was on the Upper West Side, in the nineties, near Central Park. Diplomas hung on the wall above a desk. Freud's works, the Hogarth Press Standard Edition, sat in faded blue jackets behind glass doors in an antique bookcase, and there was a fainting couch for patients in analysis, a touch taken from Freud's Vienna consulting room. The doctor sat in the corner, near the window, writing notes in a pad. I sat in the middle of the room, in an armchair. The upholstery was frayed. The doctor warned me that I was in danger, and that damage and harm would accrue and intensify. She meant brain trauma. She told me that if I stayed out of the hospital I would die.

Later that week, on a Friday, I called a car and asked the driver to take me to 168th Street and Broadway. On the drive, I phoned Regan, my father, and my friends, and told them where I was going. Like many active alcoholics, my father had an undeveloped concept of psychology. He told me, though, that he had called a psychiatrist in Fort Worth, and that the doctor had assured him that I would be in good hands. I told my father that I hoped that the doctors had all the king's horses and all the king's men.

I felt calmer in the car than I had at home. I breathed more easily. It was a clear day. The Hudson River was on the left, and I could see the George Washington Bridge ahead in the distance. The trees in Riverside Park were green. Cyclists rode on the bike path beside the highway. I hadn't planned; I'd taken some things, my keys, some cash, but not much. I'd stopped writing and reading long before, and hadn't bothered with a book.

The car stopped in front of a building made of stone. I saw doctors, nurses, and ambulances. There was the emergency room. I paid the driver, got out of the car, and walked toward the entrance. Five weeks before, an eternity before, coming down the stairs in my socks, down from the roof, I had had the feeling—it was a sense of my future, perhaps—that there was more to come, more and worse, and that I would be put away, always and forever.

I remember waiting in the emergency room. I sat bowed over, my head in my hands and my elbows on my knees. Eventually a nurse came and took me to a door that had a policeman standing outside. It was a wooden door. This was the psychiatric emergency room. The policeman knocked on the door, and a second policeman, waiting inside, opened it.

The psych ER wasn't a big space. There was a reception desk, an area with five or six cots, and a few small, private rooms. One was mine. It had a small, hard bed. Anne was on duty. She told me that she was glad that I was there, but that it might take a few days to get a room. Then Regan arrived. She sat with me while I signed the papers granting the hospital the right to hold and keep me, even against my wishes, were it necessary for my safety or the safety of others. Then it was time for her to go. I curled up on the bed. There was always a policeman nearby. I wore a hospital gown. I ate the food, swallowed the pills, slept, and waited for a bed on the ward.

That first night, people came. It was the middle of

the night. I was deep asleep. Hands and arms lifted my body from the bed. Then I was going somewhere, moving through hallways. Was I in a wheelchair? Sometimes my eyes were open. I heard voices and machine noises. A voice said, "He can go back now." I learned in the morning that I'd had a CAT scan.

I remember a woman. She looked like she was my age, in her mid-forties. She had long red hair. Her husband had driven her to the hospital from their home in the Catskills. She had dark rings around her eyes. She'd nearly died of suicide. We talked, and I told her that I hoped she'd stay in the hospital. Should she commit to treatment? What would happen? How long would she have to stay? She wanted to go home. Might she be all right at home? I suggested that she stay and be safe. It's possible that I was trying to believe that I was safe. Maybe, had she made the choice that I made, the choice to submit to life as a patient—maybe then we both would have felt less forsaken. We could be allies. But her husband came to get her, and they left.

The next morning, Monday morning, Anne told me that a room had come free, and a while later a man arrived with a wheelchair. I sat in the wheelchair, and a policeman opened the door to the general emergency room. The man behind the wheelchair pushed me through the hospital. We went up in an elevator, and then across a skywalk to another building, and from that building across another skywalk to the New York State Psychiatric Institute, a place I'd never heard of. We went into an elevator, and got off on the fifth floor. At the end of the hallway was a door. The door was made of steel, like the one in the Brooklyn hospital, and had a small window. A nurse inside unlocked the door, and the man rolled me onto the ward. He held out papers for the nurse. I recall that the nurse was Nurse D. She was head nurse.

I stood up from the chair, and Nurse D showed me around. She showed me the nurses' station; the medication dispensary; the activity rooms; the dining room; the little gym with a stationary bike; the telephones; the quiet room, empty except for a mattress on the floor, where patients can cry or rest undisturbed; and the medical examination room; and the patients' common room—everything except our bedrooms, down a hallway that was locked in the morning, and kept locked until after dinner. We were not allowed to linger in our beds. The common room was furnished with sofas and chairs, and a television that blared, and a computer for patients' use. I spent many days lying on a sofa. I had a canvas bag, and every day I carried personal items, a sweater for when the air conditioning got cold, a toothbrush and toothpaste for when my mouth got dry. The bag was black.

I used it as my pillow. I wasn't reading. I took my glasses off and put them on a table, and then stretched out on a sofa and tried to sleep. Every twenty minutes, throughout the day and night, a nurse counted us, all the patients, noting our locations, checking on us. Were we safe? Anything sharp was forbidden. Sharp objects were known as sharps. Patients who cut themselves on a sharp, or who showed, as it were, active engagement in dying, who somehow managed what the hospital called an attempt, were shadowed, everywhere they went, and at all times, by an attendant. The attendant will not leave the patient's side, even when the patient is sleeping. The practice is known as constant observation. We called it CO. I have heard of nurses tying themselves to their patients with pieces of string, just as a precaution.

Twice a day, a nurse called out, "Fresh air!" This was when we left the ward and went downstairs to sit or smoke or walk around in a yard. The yard was circled with tall chain-link fencing, and had a patio with a picnic table. You could see the George Washington Bridge to the north. It was a struggle for me to go outside, just as it had been a struggle to leave my apartment, and I often stayed upstairs. I could look out the windows.

The hospital itself, at 1051 Riverside Drive, is a modern building, clad in green-tinted glass. It has the shape of a boat. It is not a tall building, but you can glimpse it, right behind the trees lining the West Side Highway, if you look closely as you drive past. There were several wards at the Institute, one dedicated to schizophrenia and other strong psychotic illnesses, another for residents of the surrounding neighborhood, another for children and adolescents. The ward that I was on was called the General Clinical Research Unit, or GCRU. The mission of the Institute is research, and many of the patients in the GCRU were volunteers for clinical trials of new treatments. We were a broad mix of people with chronic or acute psychotic symptoms, eating disorders, and heroin addictions. The addicts had come to get clean, and to perform cognitive testing. We all had blood pressure tests, blood draws, weight checks, physical checkups, medications, counseling with our doctors, conversations and walks through the corridors with nurses, and visits from family and friends. I think that there might have been about twenty-five of us in the GCRU. I was not on a research protocol. I was a clinical patient, admitted because I was in need. There were a handful of us with clinical status, and we became a circle within the larger group, wishing each other well, consoling, checking up, hoping for happy outcomes, saying good luck when it was time for one of us to discharge, good luck, good luck out in the world.

I recall a woman in her twenties called Sarah. She seemed listless and enervated, and often sat without moving. She spoke in a monotone whisper. She confided that she had survived suicide several times, and been in and out of hospitals since she was twelve, when her parents divorced. I don't recall anyone visiting but her father. Was her mother alive? Sarah and her father sat at board games, hunched over the table.

Thomas was young too. He'd come from a southern state, and was taking Prozac. He was anxious, agitated. Shortly before he was to leave the hospital and return to his family, he was placed on CO. Nurses sat beside him on sofas, and in the dining room while he ate. A nurse sat beside his bed at night.

And there was Kathy. Kathy was my age and single. She lived on disability assistance, and did not hold a job. Like Sarah, and like Thomas, she had few visitors. She and I sat together. Her conversation was limited to illness and its consequences. She frightened me; they all did, with their stories of past admissions, drug loads and side effects, their perilous lives. Would I become one of them? Did I belong among them? Had I always belonged among the sick—ever since the night I was born, when my grandmother took me from my mother, wasn't fed her milk, wasn't given touch? What happens to children who are neglected? We don't understand, as children, that our loneliness and lack of care will become a fate—a loneliness that we will feel all our lives.

My doctor's name was Dr. A. He was in his mid-thirties. He wore a tie and a white coat, and was always harried. He told me that a whole team would take up my care, doctors, nurses, residents in psychiatry, and social workers. He promised that they would get me better, that they wouldn't give up, and that I would be safe. I sat in the common room and gazed out over the Hudson. The sun was setting over New Jersey, and the river shone in the light. It was evening. Regan had come for visiting hours. She'd brought toiletries and clothes, pants and shirts, underwear and socks. Nurse D sorted the things that I could keep in my room from the things that I couldn't. What I couldn't keep, she locked away. She kept my razor.

I wouldn't have used it, I might have told you, not for suicide; and I might not have, not in those first days. I felt relief, after finally arriving on the ward, and even anticipation. I think that I felt these things because I was out of immediate danger. I was out of harm's way, as we put it—my own harm to myself. The ER had been scary and difficult, but the ward was open and light, and people were about. I could not relax my muscles, or walk a straight path down the hall, and I believed that my life was ruined and that I would be locked away, but I nonetheless could not easily die in the hospital. Maybe you've spent some time trying every day not to die, out on your own somewhere. Maybe that effort became, or has become, your work in life. Perhaps there is help from family and friends, all the people who don't quite understand that when you tell them that they will be better off with you dead, you are speaking a truth. Maybe you're alone in a room, lying on a bed, and your chest is tight and your breathing shallow; you feel afraid to move, and sleep two or three hours each night, and then wake up in fear. Maybe you pace. Maybe you keep pills in a jar or a drawer, or hidden behind a box in the closet. When I was on the roof, I was terrified of the hospital. Who isn't scared of the hospital? We know, or think we know, its histories of lobotomy, shock therapy, and mind control experiments. We know to avoid the hospital.

Most days on the ward are pretty much the same. Shortly after admitting to the Institute, after my team of doctors had looked, listened, consoled, questioned, and taken notes on me, I began an eight-week drug trial. The drug was nortriptyline, an older-generation medication that affects norepinephrine and serotonin levels, though not as dramatically or as effectively as the newer SSRIs and NSRIs, Prozac and Effexor, for instance.

Nortriptyline didn't work. One week passed, then two, then three. I developed acid reflux. Then, one night, about a month in, I experienced a kind of shift—my chest relaxed, and I felt that I could breathe more easily. I had a moment of clarity and calm. I was in the common room. The night's visitors had gone. People were watching TV. Was I getting well? I'd been so dizzy, but now I had my balance. I went to find a nurse. I wanted to tell someone what was happening. I walked with steady steps from the common room to the nurses' station, where I said that I was feeling better, that I felt a little lighter. But by the time I got back to the common room, the effect had disappeared. It was a blow. I sat on the sofa. That night passed, and then another, and then another.

Our contemporary clinical terms—affective disorder, mood disorder, unipolar depression, bipolar depression, and so forth—are taxonomic, overlapping, and minimally descriptive outside the professions that use them, though some patients feel a clinical diagnosis to be helpful. The professional psychiatric diagnostic manual, the *Diagnostic and Statistical Manual of Mental Disorders*, currently in its fifth edition, lists disorder after disorder, including suicidal behavior disorder, which is applied to people engaged in some form of self-harm, or who are experiencing suicidal ideation, or so on. A psychiatry of disorders indicates categories of the brain gone wrong; we think of medical intakes, personal histories, hospital wards, health insurance, and trial and error with medicines. Our more colloquial terms—madness, lunacy, insanity, and other everyday labels—point to what is seen, heard, felt, and imagined in society, to appearances and the disposition (caring, contemptuous, or both) of observers through history. We use these terms casually and interchangeably, without much knowing their historical origins or literal meanings. The word "lunatic," for instance, derives from *luna*, Latin for moon. People who cycle through mood changes were once thought to be under the influence of the moon. Grief, sadness, and despair are common enough experiences for most of us; they are universal states of being, painful yet transformative. But suicide, an illness with strong common symptomologies from patient to patient around the world, cannot adequately be explained in terms of grief, sadness, or despair. And Hell and the abyss? Those places don't exist outside myth and religion.

Eight weeks is a long time to sit getting worse in a hospital. Three times each week, I had psychotherapy with Dr. A. I begged for his promises that I would ride my bike again, or write a story, or survive my loss of my mother. At the end of every session, he asked me to draw a house. My houses were plain; and I can't draw anyway. So what if the walls were crooked and the windows oblong? No one was ever in those houses, no stick-figure family, no mom, no dad. My feeling that I would die, or that I would at least never leave institutions, grew stronger, and I became convinced that I was in the wrong hospital. I remember conspiring on the phone with Regan. I told her where it hurt, and insisted that I was sick in my body, not my head.

"I feel sick all over," I told her.

Sometimes I wept in the quiet room; on other days, I wept to friends on the pay phone, or talked to nurses, or looked at the computer. I wrote short notes to my friends— terrors and updates. I stretched out on a sofa and waited for the meds to calm me enough to watch the news or read a few pages of a book from the patient library, a room right outside the locked doors of the ward. The library featured works on psychiatry, and there were paperback novels, memoirs, and biographies left by previous patients.

I couldn't read much, not at a time. Moving my eyes, even to gaze around the ward, was fatiguing and painful. I took Seroquel, an antipsychotic, when the anxiety was excruciating, and the doctors kept up the Ativan. The anxiety by now had become less a matter of shaking and trembling, and more a kind of buzzing in my chest. Seroquel made me sleepy, but didn't put me to sleep. I lay still, but I wasn't still, I was vibrating. I was clumsy. I might reach for a cup, and then knock it with my hand. I might walk down the middle of the hall, and then my shoulder would brush against the wall. Sometimes I lay

like a corpse, my arms folded over my chest, just as I had
in the months before admitting to the hospital, when I
was lying on the tarp, preparing in earnest for death. At
the Institute, I sometimes jumped up and darted around
the ward. Other times, I sat still, rigid, afraid to move
or try. I asked the nurses if I would be all right. Would
I make it? I made the effort to move my jaw, my mouth
and tongue. Did the others on the ward feel as scared as I
did? Were they afraid that they'd never be well?

Visitors came at eight, mothers and fathers, brothers
and sisters, couples and single friends. The nurse let people in, locked the door, and then called our names or
came looking for us. All guests stopped at the nurses'
station, where a nurse looked inside bags and backpacks.
Some families didn't talk, but instead sat gathered around
tables, playing board games. The hospital had a closet-
ful of games. Other patients were alone during visiting
hours.

My friends and I might hug when they arrived, but
lightly, and only for an instant. We sat in the common
room. I asked about the world, and my friends talked
about their lives. I tried to describe my state to Dave and
Geneve, to Kathy and Jon, to Paul, to Jane, to Jenny, to
Nicky, to Janice, to Sasha and Vlada. But I didn't have
many words. And how were they to understand my feeling that I was dying, that I was leaving them? I felt as if

my friends were far away. I think of that remove not as a distance but as a disconnect. The disconnect felt, for want of a better way of putting it, dimensional—a disturbance in the cosmos. I have heard this sensation described as the glass wall. My friends and I occupied, it seemed, different times and places. We were sitting together, but we weren't together. They lived in historical time, not in eternal dying; they had yesterdays, and a today and a tomorrow. The world from which they'd come, and to which they would return, was lost to me.

When visiting hours were over, my friends picked up their purses and bags, and I walked them to the door. The nurse unlocked the door, and my friends went out. Sometimes I wept. I could see them through the little window. I wanted them to stay another moment, at least that. We might glance at each other through the window in the door, but then they turned, and I watched them walk down the hall.

I'd wept deeply before my time in the hospital, and have since, though never for as long during a day, or over as many days, as in the quiet room at the hospital. I went into the room, lay down on the mattress, and sobbed over my betrayal of my mother; over old loves; over my choice, when younger, to write; and over the houses that we'd lived in when I was growing up, and the friends that I made and then said goodbye to whenever we moved.

I cried over our cats Zelda, F. Scott, Justine, Pippin, the litters of kittens on blankets in boxes—so many cats. I'd held them, and slept in bed with them, and cradled them in my lap.

The nurses urged me off the mattress. They suggested groups for game-playing sessions, and leisure activity workshops. How do we find peace and pleasure in our lives? Might I try keeping a journal? Writing would promote neuronal growth and emotional insight, but I refused. It was awful to see my misshaped letters and unreadable words. I'd worked most of my life at writing; I'd been a professional, and now I couldn't bear it. Sometimes I wrote short notes on the computer. I recall an afternoon in the common room. Maybe I had been in the hospital for a month or so. The TV was on, and patients sat watching. I was lying on my back on the sofa. My head rested on the canvas bag, and my arms were crossed over my chest. It was late in the day, and, looking out the windows, I could see blue sky. I got up and walked across the room. I could sense the hair on my arms, as if blown on some faint breeze. It was a burning feeling.

Around that time, sometime in late June, I noticed that my feet and lower legs tingled and ached, and often looked blue. My nails hardened, thickened, developed ridges, and became opaque. I couldn't bite through them.

I wasn't shaving, and my beard grew stiff and wiry. I complained to Regan. Was I suffering a vascular disease? Was I suffering a rheumatologic disease? Why was I being held on a psychiatric ward? I knew the doctor's position on these questions. They understood, or knew, or simply believed that I was not making sense. How would they have thought otherwise?

"I'm not delusional," I said, over and over again to Dr. A. I told him that I knew that I was sick, but not in a way that he believed, and that I needed another kind of medicine. In order to calm me, he made an appointment with the internist on call, who crossed the skywalk from Columbia Presbyterian, read my lab reports, checked my neurological functioning, listened to my heart and my breathing, and told me that I was medically fit. I was relieved, though only for three or four minutes. I thanked the internist for his patience. I left the exam room. My chest tightened, and my arms and legs again felt leaden.

In early July, my memoir of my mother came out. I'd been on the ward for two months. There had been no time for the publishers to delay the publication. Had I been in better shape, I might have given readings, or traveled to promote the book. Maybe there would have been a publication party, and dinners. Someone brought a copy, but I didn't want to hold it. The book jacket features a picture of my mother taken in the 1950s by the photographer Joseph Steinmetz. Steinmetz had a studio in Sarasota, and took pictures of iconic Florida scenes, like tourists grilling on the beach, as well as portraits of Ringling Brothers Circus performers, including the clown Emmett Kelly.

The memoir came out around the same time that I developed eczema on my forehead. The eczema presented as a patch of reddish skin above the bridge of my nose, an itchy patch between my eyes, exactly where the mystical "third eye" appears in religious iconography and artistic imagery, and directly over the area of the brain known as the medial prefrontal cortex, which is associated with empathy, anxiety, temporal and spatial awareness, autonomous nervous system functioning, memory retention and sequencing, stability of mood, and executive functioning. The medial prefrontal cortex helps provide for what we call our humanity and our condition, our cognizance of ourselves, our competency at navigating society and the physical world, and our health and well-being under stress or under threat—the medial prefrontal cortex is crucial to proprioception, bonding with others, and our safety in the world.

Touching on the ward was not permitted. The hospital is meant to halt and reverse the effects of trauma and its aftermaths, but is governed by protocols that enforce patients' separateness from one another—a new isolation. For many who have survived alone, alone in an apartment or house, the hospital might be our first time, maybe in a long while, spent with a group, in this case a community in pain but nonetheless with memories or fantasies of wellness. In the hospital, we live among people trained to ease our crises, doctors and nurses, nutritionists, medical technicians, and social workers—the hospital can be seen as a therapeutic city, and psychiatric patients as problematic through-traffic; in sickness, we take the ward as a gulag. Some of us had been sexually or otherwise violently abused—hit, bullied, intimidated. Some of us had been left by loved ones. Some didn't know what had happened; the disease had seemed simply to *appear*, maybe during childhood, maybe in college, maybe, as with me and many men, in middle age. It is terrible for the old. Physical contact between patients was potentially traumatizing. Touch came from nurses drawing blood, or light hugs with visitors, who, when saying goodbye, seemed eager to go. I wanted to leave with my friends, if only to have dinner with them, something over on Broadway, a few blocks east.

I could not have made it to Broadway. Had I stumbled, beltless, in my socks or unlaced shoes down the hall, I surely would have run back and banged on the door. Had my friends helped me escape, make a break for it, I nonetheless wouldn't have gone far. I could not have held a menu and calmly chosen what to eat, or picked up a glass without spilling, or held a knife and fork without trembling. I could not easily swallow; my jaw hurt, and my mouth was dry from medications. I could not have joined the conversation, only made people nervous. Dining out, driving a car, making coffee—these things were not possible. They were unsafe. Everything outside the ward was unsafe. My apartment was unsafe. The subway was unsafe. The street was unsafe. Back in the spring, in April, I'd left the Brooklyn hospital and passed in an instant from shelter to exposure. On one side of the steel door, I'd felt competent, ready to resume my life. On the other side of the door, I was frightened and lost.

Once we called hospitals asylums. An asylum is a refuge, a place away from harm. That word is no longer used to describe the hospital, unless in a derogatory fashion; we might call the hospital a psych ward, and yet imagine it as a crumbling home for degenerates, or a maze of hallways where halfway naked people sit. The word "asylum" describes the institution, the hospital; but in another, perhaps fuller sense, asylum is a provision. Asylum can be legislated and granted. Refugees, political prisoners, those persecuted over race or their way of life might find asylum in a church, a new country, an international airport, or any hidden place. Children bullied at school may find asylum at home, but for children abused in the home, there is no asylum. Society allows victims of violence in marriages and partnerships little protection. Soldiers in battle have no safety from war, only weaponry, their training, and their trust in each other; and the survivors, the returning, the lucky ones, often struggle to recover from war's effects, and many die of suicide. Who shelters the victims of rape? Grave psychotic illness has one refuge. "Why won't they take me to the right hospital? There's nothing wrong with my brain. I need to be in a regular hospital! They're going to kill me!" I cried to Regan, and begged her to tell the doctors that they were making a mistake.

"They won't listen to me! They think I'm crazy!" I shouted into the phone, over and over again.

"You're not crazy," Regan might say; and eventually she did phone my doctor. She talked to him more than once.

But we were also fighting.

"Are you talking to her? Why is she coming to see you? Why do you let her?" Regan shouted through the phone. She meant my ex-girlfriend Fran, with whom I'd cheated during the lead-up to hospitalization, and who both visited and called. "She's worried about me," I said. "She is afraid for me." I told Regan that Fran and I were not in resurgence.

"How is this supposed to make me feel?" Regan cried. I didn't know how to answer. I wanted to hear from anyone, anyone at all, who could visit or call. Now I realize how scared Regan must have been, and how much she must have felt my psychosis, maybe felt it as hers; and I wonder whether she was not rebuking me so much as trying to save herself.

Regan, and my friends who visited the ward and then returned to the outside, and my colleagues, my publisher and editor, the people I depended on and who depended on me, would no longer want or need me; I was certain of this; it seemed inevitable. I would never write again—that was over. "I ruin everything," I told everyone, my friends in New York, and the ones who came from out of town. Some came often, and others were scared to visit, but came anyway. They sat across from me. They were furtive, exasperated, wanting to go, wanting to flee, not knowing what to do with their hands, smiling too much, forcing calm expressions, making sympathetic faces, posing. My nails were yellow and thick. My hands shook. My skin was itchy, and my hair was growing out. I was unshaved. My beard grew down my neck.

"You haven't ruined anything! Don't say that!"

"I've ruined myself."

"Donald."

"I have."

"Donald."

"Look at me! Can't you see what I *am*?"

Every night at nine, after visitors were gone, safe out-side, the nurses unlocked the dormitory. This was when I took my night meds. The med nurse was older, and kind. He had good words for us. "Here you go," he said. For sleep, I took Trazodone, Ativan, Seroquel, nortriptyline, and chloral hydrate, which came into use as a sedative in the nineteenth century. I drank it as syrup. It came in a shallow plastic cup topped with a tear-away foil lid. After swallowing meds, I might sit in the common room and talk to Kathy about her own medication, or about what it was like to live on disability. I asked Thomas when he might go home. Was his Prozac working? How long had he been taking it? What else might the doctors give him? How long had he felt suicidal? When had that begun? When would his family come to visit?

Nighttime was when I felt best. In bed, I waited. These were my only moments, the twenty or thirty minutes before sleep, as the medications began to work, my only times of anything like peace. At the beginning of my stay, I had a roommate. He was young, in his early thirties. His face was scarred, as if slashed with a knife. We had our beds and dressers, and a bathroom with a shower. My face in the bathroom mirror looked gray. I could see the circles around my eyes. Beside the bed-

room door, and running the length of the door, an outside curtain covered a strip of unbreakable glass. Every
twenty minutes, throughout the night, a nurse pulled
the curtain aside to peek in at us. Were we breathing?
Had we found a way to die? Doorknobs were narrow
and thin, rather than bulbous; there was no way to hang
a knotted sheet. No nails showed in the furniture. My
roommate was nervous, aggressive; he moved in bursts.
I was uncomfortable around him, though I never felt in
danger. Maybe he needed a friend. We didn't talk, and
I never learned his history, though it seemed to me that
he'd suffered some great and lasting violence. That was
what I felt—I felt his past, you could say, and my own.
Later in my stay, I was moved to a single room at the
end of the hall.

I slept two, three hours, and then woke. Sometimes
I got up and stumbled down the hall to the nurses' station, where I asked for more Seroquel. Then back to
bed for a few more hours before waking again, startled,
early in the morning, when the medical residents and
daytime staff arrived. I could hear their footsteps and
their voices. Patients lined up for blood pressure and
weight checks. Sometimes a nurse or a resident took me
into the medical examination office and drew blood. I
clenched my fist. The nurse searched for a vein—tap,
tap, tap on my arm. When the nurse couldn't find a

vein, I felt relieved and scared. It usually took a minute. The nurse cleaned the skin with a cotton pad. I could smell the rubbing alcohol—the smell of going to the doctor. "Just a little pinch." It usually took one poke, and then another and another, before the vial started filling. I watched blood seep into the vial, and then looked away. The nurse popped one vial cartridge out of the hypodermic chamber and inserted the next. I felt the needle moving beneath my skin. When would it end? I needed the procedure to be over. I was sweaty and breathing quickly. The nurse taped a cotton swab over my skin.

"All done."

Couldn't the doctors see, in my blood work, signs of my real disease? There was nothing wrong with my thinking. Surely I wasn't psychotic. Surely I wasn't hallucinating. I thought I had a vascular disease. Why else would my extremities tingle and ache? Or I had a muscular disorder, some sort of dystrophy. Why else was I so clumsy and stiff? Did I have a rare disease affecting the bones of my face? Why else would I see, as I did, or thought I did one day, my misshapen skull in the bathroom mirror? It was fleeting, a moment of death imagined. I stood before the mirror, and saw my hair, ears, beard, and my chin and mouth, my cloudy eyes. But my cheekbones and jaw looked warped and disfigured. My cheeks jutted out, and

I thought I saw, for a moment, my eye sockets in place of my eyes.

I ran from my room, down the hall, not able to keep straight, careening, furious, scared. Was it morning? Was it nighttime? And when was it that I stormed the nurses' station? It was a day near the end of my medication trial, a day in July. Why hadn't I already been taken by ambulance to the right hospital? Why was I being held against my will? Why would no one listen to me? Why would no one help me? I was pleading. I was begging. I don't remember if I was shouting. Who would hear me? Who would believe me?

Dr. A was standing behind the desk. He stepped back. Immediately the area filled with personnel. Nurses and residents and social workers appeared and formed a line; they made a kind of semicircle. They were ready to tackle and restrain me. "Stop right there," my doctor said to me, and I stopped. Were the other patients watching? Would I be put in a straitjacket? Dr. A held his hands out, palms facing me, as if he were pushing something away. Then he turned his hands palm down. "Take it easy," he said. No one moved. The doctor gently lowered, and then raised, and then lowered his hands. I stepped back. I looked down at the floor. Had he really thought that I'd become violent? He dropped his hands, and I went into the common room and lay on the sofa. I felt misunderstood, and I was ashamed.

A few days later, Dr. A brought me into the dining room. It was midday. The tables had been pushed to the walls. My team of doctors and the nurses and residents in psychiatry sat in a line, like a jury. There were the social workers, the ones who'd encouraged me to join in activities that I rejected. I didn't want to play games with patients who got excited and noisy, or eat the donuts that the nurses brought. I didn't want to sit in the leisure activity workshop and hear about pleasures that I would never feel, relaxing on porches or going on vacations or having picnics. I couldn't bear the weekly cooking class that was held in the little kitchen down the hall from the dining room. Must I fumble with pans? I couldn't safely boil water. I'd once been a good home cook. I had cooked in my own kitchen. I had chopped vegetables with the Sabatier knife that my father had held to my mother. I had cooked with girlfriends, and read literature, and gone to movies, and acted in plays, and graduated from schools, and run errands, and sat with my mother while she shook from delirium tremens, and driven with my grandfather, her father, through the North Carolina mountains, where he and my grandmother retired. My grandfather and I used to go for milk from a farm in Old Fort that had one cow. He was in his eighties, and I was in my thirties. He took Lasix for his congested heart, and fre-

quently stopped the car to urinate in the bushes beside
the road. On one of our drives, he asked if I'd been to
the Carl Sandburg house, outside Hendersonville, and I
said, "No, I haven't," and so we drove across the mountain to see the poet's house and the land around it, the
woods and the barn and the pens that hold the descen-
dants of the goats that Sandburg kept. Lying in bed,
the night after my grandfather died of a heart attack, in
1995, I had the feeling that he'd driven to Brooklyn in
his Buick and was waiting for me to come downstairs
to the sidewalk and get in. I didn't go to the window to
look. The next day I flew to North Carolina to scatter
his ashes. I'd been in therapy, by then, for twelve years,
since my mother had got sober, when I lived on the
Upper East Side, not long after I came to New York.
My apartment then was across from a fire station. My
roommate was an actor named Scott. My bedroom was
through the kitchen. The bedroom had a sleeping loft
with a ladder, and was painted white—white ceiling,
white walls, and white floor. I put my desk under the
loft, and wrote stories on a Smith Corona typewriter.
When I hit the return key, the recoil force of the electric carriage jarred the typewriter, and with each new
line of writing, the typewriter inched farther sideways
across the desk. Day and night, I could hear the fire
trucks across the street, their sirens.

In 1983, a friend, Susan, whose mother had died of suicide, referred me to my first therapist. His name was D, and he had come to New York from the Midwest, where he'd been a Congregationalist minister. D told me that he'd become a therapist because he had felt unable to help his parishioners, only offer homilies and consolations. He worked out with weights, and had a bowl haircut. His office was in a brownstone, three blocks uptown from my apartment, on the second floor in the back. D said that if I drank I would become an alcoholic like my parents. I went to Al-Anon. Al-Anon is for people whose lives have been affected by alcoholics, family members, for instance. The meetings stem from Alcoholics Anonymous, which got its start in 1935, at a house in Akron, Ohio, where two men who believed themselves incurable alcoholics sat through a day and a night, keeping each other company, telling their stories. One was a doctor named Bob, the other a stockbroker named Bill. Bill and Doctor Bob realized that if they could stay sober for a day, a single day, then maybe they could do it again, and from that came the main lesson of AA, that sobriety can only be undertaken with others, one day at a time. Alcoholics Anonymous helped produce the concept of alcoholism as a disease, not a sin or a sign of weakness, and this understanding has led to better health care and reduced stigma. Stigma, the stigmata, refers to Christ's martyrdom, His blood, the wounds made by the nails driven through His hands and feet when He is crucified by the Romans; and on His head, the marks left by the crown of thorns that Christ wore as He died. Christ dies for our sins. He dies to save us. I read and reread the Twelve Steps of AA, which follow from our acceptance of some higher power in our lives, *God, as we understood Him*. At night, I called my mother, and we talked about the program. At that time, I was beginning as a writer. The short stories that I wrote then were about her, mainly, but one was about a man I met one night on the street, not long before I started therapy with D.

I was on my way home from a party where I'd had a lot to drink. The man was waving a flashlight, looking to open the sidewalk grate to get at the fuse box in the basement. The street was dark, and there were no people. The power had gone out in the man's building. But the sidewalk grate was locked, and he asked me to help him upstairs to his room. His name was Waldo. He was German, had gray hair, and looked sick. His building was a neglected rooming house a block east of Park Avenue. Waldo's flashlight lit the way up the stairs. The light was dim, and I heard noises coming from behind doors on the hallway. Waldo's room was on the second floor; it had a table, two chairs, and a single bed. The bathroom was down the hall, but Waldo had a sink. The room's one window was partly covered by a torn shade hanging from its spindle. Waldo lit a candle. A little refrigerator held cans of beer with their lids popped open. Waldo told me that he didn't like fizzy American beer; he liked the beer that he'd drunk in Germany when he was young. Snapshots were pinned on the wall, and a medal hung from a nail. It was Waldo's Iron Cross, his EK2, he said. He told me that he'd been one of the boy recruits conscripted by Himmler to fill out the Nazi ranks at the end of World War II. EK2 medals were given to soldiers who fought on the Eastern Front. I watched him in the candlelight. He told me that he'd finished the war in a prison camp, and that in America he'd been a baker. He showed me pictures of his trip with his wife to Florida in the sixties, and then raised his shirt, displaying gunshot wounds. He asked me to get him a pistol. He had no one, he told me. He was alone. He said that he wanted to shoot himself. Would I help him? Could I bring him a gun? I told him that I didn't have a gun, and couldn't get one, and then I got up to go. He tried to stop me. He grabbed my arm, but I pulled away. "Get me a gun, get me a gun," he pleaded. I ran down the stairs and up the street. I saw him after that, a few times, looking out from behind his shade. I hurried past.

Back when I was a teenager, I liked to visit my father's mother and his alcoholic brother, my uncle, Eldridge,

also known as Bob, and sometimes Sam. This was in the
mid-1970s, after my family left Virginia for Miami. I rode
the bus across the Everglades and up the coast to Sarasota,
where Eldridge and his mother, my other grandmother,
shared a house on a man-made lake. The house was west
of town, about a twenty-minute drive from my mother's
parents' house. The land out there was scrubby and dry.
Eldridge kept a stack of *Playboys* and a gun collection. He
ate in the middle of the night, watching Johnny Carson.
My grandmother was frail, and had white hair. Her name
was Eliza. She and Eldridge lived together until she died,
in the mid-1980s. A few years later, at fifty-one, he died
from alcohol poisoning. When I was a teenager, I thought
that my uncle was a free spirit. One night when I was fifteen, he threw me onto the foldout sofa on the enclosed
porch, the Florida room. I thought that he was wrestling.
He climbed on top of me, pinning me down on the mattress. I was on my stomach, and he lay across my back. I
smelled his English Leather cologne and the beer on his
breath. Was he playing? It didn't feel like playing. What
was happening? What would he do? He didn't move. I
felt his weight on me. Did he have an erection? I said,
"Get off," and then, again, "Get off." He rolled over and
lay beside me. How long had we lain like that? Why did
my uncle put his weight on me like that? I felt terrified;
I felt that I was in danger, and that I must run away, and

that I would never be able to see him again. It happened in a moment. And I understand now why our grandmother, when Terry and I were little, when we were four, five, six, took us into her bed to sleep. She was protecting us from our grandfather. His name was Robert Antrim. He was a retired farmer, taciturn and unsmiling. He wandered around the house wearing Old Spice and his underwear. He died when I was twelve. The morning after that night in Sarasota, the night my uncle got on top of me, I fled to Miami, and a month later left home for school in Virginia. I returned to Florida less and less over the years, except to care for my mother.

I was twenty-three, twenty-four, and twenty-five. I went to therapy with D, and then, three years after he left the city, in 1988, I began again, with a man named R. R had come from England to study at the William Alanson White Institute, on the Upper West Side. He and I met twice a week in an attic room. I rode the 86th Street bus across Central Park. Sometimes, when coming into the room, I might say hello and ask R how he'd been, and he might then ask me what it would mean to me to know. We tangled over whether I needed to talk about my father. The William Alanson White Institute practices interpersonal relations, which examines the family and society—the patient's story of growing up and living in the world—in relation to trauma, broken bonds, and compromised lives.

Harry Stack Sullivan, the White Institute's first director, introduced the term "problems of living," economically expressing the idea that anxiety originates in crises and failures in relationships, in violations of trust. Problems of living include crises and concerns of daily life—divorce, the death of a family member, bankruptcy—problems that are not necessarily associated with suicide, but that are, just the same, frequently causative. Sullivan's name was unfortunately taken by a sex cult, the Sullivanians, who lived at that time in a brownstone twenty blocks north and west of the White Institute, between Broadway and Riverside Drive. I recall walking past their building one afternoon in the late 1980s. At that time, when I was around thirty, I was reading sociology and child psychiatry. I read John Bowlby, whose work on separation and loss forms attachment theory, which predicts social competency and the ability to thrive as functions of nurturing early attachments, of bonding; and Erik Erikson, whose work suggests that the violation of the child's trust leads to a life of increasingly perilous failures of trust; and D. W. Winnicott, the British pediatrician whose writings stress the importance of parental love, the ongoing connection between mother and child. All these authors describe the crucial role of touch, and of the family setting as a place of safety and security.

After leaving therapy with R, in 1991, I began with

M. I moved to Brooklyn, to the apartment from which I ran to the roof. M grew up in Staten Island. She had her office in an Art Deco apartment building on York Avenue in Manhattan, near the East River. I commuted from Brooklyn to Manhattan to see her, sometimes once a week, sometimes twice. Our therapy lasted fifteen years. During those years, I published a novel that begins and ends with a man who is alone and looking out a window, and whose wife transforms into a prehistoric fish; and then a novel about a host of brothers who have lost their father, and who rampage through their immense, ancient library; and then one about a psychoanalyst who, when a colleague lifts him in a bear hug, levitates to the ceiling of a pancake house. M followed Heinz Kohut, a German immigrant who practiced what he called self psychology, which emphasizes the integrity and wholeness of the self, whatever that is.

After writing three novels and the memoir of my life with my mother, I began filling Klonopin prescriptions from the Brooklyn psychiatrist, the doctor who scribbled the graph showing depression on one side of a line, anxiety on the other. I had survived, or thought that I'd survived, my parents' drinking and shouting, our constant moving, the losses of places and friends, my uncle lying on my back, annihilation after annihilation. I'd played in the yard, and smashed tennis balls against walls for hours, and built model airplanes, and listened to my records at night in my room. I'd slept at night with cats for company, and ridden my bike, and struggled in school, and, later in life, gone to bars, and then quit going to bars, and smoked cigarettes and pot, and fallen in love, and argued and made up, and refused to speak to my father, and suffered my mother. None of this had stopped my dying. Writing had not stopped my dying. The Twelve Steps had not stopped my dying. Therapy alone hadn't stopped it, and my old friends couldn't, nor could Regan. No one could.

Dr. A waited in the patients' dining room. Nurse D was there. The activity leaders were there. It was mid-summer, and I'd not been outside for weeks. I'd had no fresh air. My medication trial was ending. My book had come out, and I'd seen my face disfigured in the bathroom mirror. I had charged the nurses' station. Now my doctors, my team, sat in a circle, holding notebooks and pens. The tables where patients ate meals had been pushed against the walls. In the center of the dining room was a chair. One person in the room I did not recognize, a woman wearing a Chanel suit. Her hair was cut short. She spoke directly and deliberately, and immediately I was terrified of her.

"You are sick," she said.

I cried and cried.

"You are psychotic."

I sobbed, "No, no."

"We can get you better."

Tears ran down my face, onto my clothes.

"We can get you well," she said.

Her name was Dr. P, and she was an ECT specialist at the Institute. ECT, electroconvulsive therapy, once known as shock therapy, produces convulsions that affect dopamine and other neurotransmitters. During the procedure, the patient is anesthetized, and paralytic drugs are administered to quiet convulsions in the body. The focus of treatment is the brain. Without paralytics, the patient will twitch and flail on the operating table. ECT is a powerful measure against suicide, and yet it has traditionally been used as a treatment of last resort. Early images of patients undergoing shock therapy inform our fears. I was terrified of ECT. I imagined the electric chair; and I knew, or thought I knew, what shock would do to me. It would destroy my ability to write, or even to think clearly. It would take away my memories and my personality. I would be unable to function, and live confined to hospital wards.

"We want to perform ECT. It is an excellent treatment. There is nothing to be afraid of. ECT will not harm you. It will help you. We need you to agree. We need your consent."

Who could save me? I wandered around the ward,

crying. I asked one of the residents if she would ever do ECT herself, and she told me that if she were as sick as I was, she would.

Later that day, or maybe it was the next day, the patients' phone rang. It was for me. It was the writer David Foster Wallace. I'd met David, but didn't know him. I'd read his writing; his frantically paced stories about manic, destructive characters; his funny and digressive, intimate nonfiction pieces; and the novel *Infinite Jest*. Suicide features as a concern in much of Wallace's work. He told me, that day on the phone, that our mutual friend Jon had shared the news about my situation. Did I mind hearing from him?

"No, I don't mind," I said, and he asked how I was feeling.

"Not so good."

"How long have you been there?"

"Two months."

He said, "I'm calling to tell you that if your doctors recommend ECT, then I want you to do it."

He asked me, "Have they offered it?"

"Yes," I said.

David told me that he'd had ECT in the Midwest, twenty years before, during the eighties. He said that ECT could save my life, that it is a safe and robust treatment, that the doctors knew what they were doing, and that I should not be afraid that I would lose my memory or competency; I was in good hands. "I want you to try ECT," he told me. He said it again and again, because he knew that I was ruminating, and that I would not be able to believe him for long, just a few minutes.

"Tell me one more time?" I asked. I didn't want him to go. He stayed on the phone with me a long time. When we said goodbye, I dialed Regan, and said, "I'm going to have ECT."

"You are?"

I told Regan about David's sudden appearance, about his story, and the sound of his voice, his encouragement; and then, after Regan and I hung up, I went looking for my doctor; and a day or two later, early in the morning, a nurse came to my door. She had my medical charts. She gave me a hospital gown. I put on my socks, pants, and the gown, and we walked through the ward. The nurse unlocked the main door, and we went to a room down the hall. It was an operating room—lots of medical equipment, but also computers and electronics.

You lie in your gown and your socks on the table. You're looking up at the white ceiling. The ECT nurse glues electrodes to your head, chest, arms, and legs. Wires run from the electrodes, across your body. You nod to the anesthesiologist—they're usually pretty friendly—who sticks you with a needle, beginning the IV. Maybe you speak to the administering physician, the team leader. This doctor stands behind you, behind your head, programming the shock. You look up at the doctor's face. The ECT nurse fits an oxygen meter over your index finger, and then binds your ankle with a blood pressure cuff. The cuff will remain inflated throughout the procedure. It blocks the paralytic, succinylcholine, from entering your foot. This allows your toes to twitch, visible evidence of convulsion. Vital-signs monitors beep. You are having right unilateral ECT. The convulsion should last half a minute. If other patients are doing ECT, your buddies on the ward, then you might glimpse one or two asleep on gurneys in the recovery area. You feel something like fellowship, as if you were all at war together, or had been in the same dreadful accident. You ask the ECT nurse to hold your hand, and you squeeze hard. The anesthesiologist says, "Atropine." You are crying. You've been in tears the whole time. Atropine keeps the heart beating. You tell the doctors that you want to get better. You've only ever wanted to get better. There is a bite plate on the metal table beside the anesthesiologist. The nurse fits the oxygen mask over your face. The anesthesiologist inserts a syringe into the pipette connected to the needle in your arm. The anesthetic trickles down the tube. You can smell it. It has a sweet smell. You count backwards, one hundred, ninety-nine, ninety-eight, and then the anesthetic reaches your blood, and a second passes, and you feel that you are falling—and then blackness. The succinylcholine goes in, and you no longer breathe on your own; you are on life-support, and your body will not shudder or shake. And now you are awake—did anything happen? Are we ready to begin? A voice asks you where you are, and you reply to the voice that you are in the General Clinical Research Unit, on the fifth floor of the New York State Psychiatric Institute, at 1051 Riverside Drive, in Manhattan. You are behind a curtain, recovering in bed. Your mouth is dry. You feel like you could sleep. You have had general anesthesia. Your friends in treatment have already woken and been returned to the ward; and, in fact, you are done; it is over.

"How are you feeling?"

It was the nurse, the one who earlier that morning had knocked on my bedroom door and brought me to the ECT room. She held my arm, steadied me while I stood, and we walked back to the ward, where there was breakfast. I sat alone in the dining room. I had oatmeal, and drank milk and coffee. It was midmorning. I ate my oatmeal, and then the nurse helped me down the hall. ECT patients could go to their rooms after treatment. I lay in bed and wondered if I felt better. Had anything changed? Maybe I slept. I looked forward to feeling well. I couldn't recall feeling well, or imagine what that might be like.

Our parents' marriage went into crisis for the first time when Terry was five and I was six. We were living in Gainesville, Florida, where my father was finishing graduate school, at the University of Florida. We lived in a small, wood-frame house at the top of a dead-end road. Spanish moss hung from the trees, and there were always kids out playing. My friends and I went on expeditions to a pond at the end of the road. The pond seemed far from home, a trek, though it was only a few backyards away. Algae on top made the pond bright green. The water beneath was murky and smelly. Trees lined the far perimeter, and fallen branches, partly submerged, looked like alligators. Dragonflies hovered, and little fish surfaced and then went back underwater. I had a toy pistol that shot paper caps. I collected tadpoles in jars and took them home. They always died. There was a girl who lived across from us. She was about twelve. She babysat Terry and me. I had a crush on her, and imagined scenes in which she was in peril, and I was able to rescue her. My parents threw parties, and my sister and I couldn't sleep, and in the morning we found their graduate school friends passed out on chairs and the living room floor. Twenty years later, after she got sober, after she stopped blacking out, my mother told me about my father's affair. His lover was an assistant professor in the French Department at the university, a poet who, according to my mother, later married a man who abused her. My mother told me that before she and my father separated, I'd again and again pressed my face against the floor, and then rubbed my nose and forehead into the carpet until I had sores. How miserable I must have been. I was five. I'll never forget my parents' violent fights. My mother told me that her parents had been drunks when she'd been a child, and that her mother threw water in her face to stop her crying, and put bourbon in her baby formula, dosing her to sleep. Bourbon was my mother's drink. She drank Jim Beam, or, sometimes, Kentucky Gentleman.

Shock treatment for suicide wasn't always induced electrically, not until the early 1940s. Electroshock therapy proceeded from insulin, camphor, and Metrazol shock therapies, a line of hormonal and chemical treatments that sometimes showed positive results, but that caused anxiety and discomfort, both for patients and for their administering doctors, who worried that the therapy might kill, which, though rarely, it did. Insulin shock was developed and promoted by Manfred Sakel, an Austrian. It went into use in the early 1930s. The patient was given increasing doses of insulin, reducing blood sugar and producing coma and seizures. Old film reels show insulin shock patients trembling and quivering. Many treatments were required, and Sakel's patients undertook it daily, which must have been grueling. Sakel proclaimed insulin shock therapy as a cure for schizophrenia and other historically intractable psychotic illnesses, and even drug addictions. Sakel was unrealistic; nonetheless, insulin shock was used in Europe and America until the 1950s, when it gave way to electroshock therapy, a safer and, as it were, cleaner, more effective procedure. Electroshock was introduced in 1941 by the Italian neurologist Ugo Cerletti, after animal experimentation.

ECT was administered three mornings a week, Monday, Wednesday, and Friday. Would it work? And if not, then what came next? The doctors added lithium to my drug load. Lithium slows metabolism. My weight increased, and my movement and speech slowed. I searched for words, even the answers to simple questions. "Uh, uh, uh," I would say before beginning sentences. A week went by, and then two, and then three: one treatment, and then two treatments, and then three, four, five. I had ten rounds of ECT, or maybe eleven. The anesthesiologist told me that the doctors wouldn't give up. "We'll take care of you," he said, and then told me that he had once been averse to electroconvulsive therapy, thinking it barbaric, but had been persuaded to come across the skywalk from neurosurgery and observe. He said that he'd watched patients improve and go home. The ECT doctor recalibrated the shock. We kept going. Patients discharged, and new patients arrived on the ward. John came one morning in a wheelchair. John was my age. He'd been transferred from another hospital. He looked sick and wretched in his gown. He wasn't registering much. Dawn came late at night. She was on a gurney, tranquilized, breathing slowly, her stiletto heels piled on top of the sheet covering her.

For her first days, Dawn did not leave the quiet room. She wore her hospital gown, and did not speak. She was thirty, and had been an artist, and had acted in experimental theater. She'd grown up in New York, and was an only child. She described herself as manic-depressive, bipolar, and said that she'd been in a manic turn when they brought her in. I never learned what had happened. She and I sat in the common room with John, whose beard grew down his neck. He'd swallowed Klonopin tablets that he'd sorted out of his monthly prescriptions. It had taken him months to save enough. I saw in his life what I feared for my own. He'd been married, but there were no children. His father had been a doctor, and John said that such close proximity to childhood images added to his difficulty on the ward. This wasn't his first hospitalization. There was no family, or maybe there was a sister. He was a banker, but out of work. On weekends, he drove out to Long Island, where he was building a house that he couldn't complete. He saw only sitting in his house on Long Island Sound, all by himself.

And there was Helen. Helen came to the Institute in late July. She was eighty, or older, catatonic, stooped over from the pain in her muscles and joints. She pressed her arms against her sides, and her hands and fingers were clenched. She couldn't look up, or eat much, and she barely spoke. She moved very little, but she did not seem still. She began ECT immediately after admitting. Sometimes, before bedtime, Dawn and I huddled on the sofa. We sat close, though not so close that a nurse might see and then stop us. Sometimes we touched hands. The television blared. Dawn and I whispered about other patients, about our families and our childhoods, about what we did on the outside. Her parents came to visit, and I met them.

I met my stepmother the first time at the airport. It must've been 1983. I was living on the Upper East Side. My mother had been two or maybe three times at Mercy Hospital, in Coral Gables, for alcohol poisoning. She would stop drinking or die, the doctors told her, and my father picked up and left. They were getting divorced again. Not long after my father left my mother, he called from Miami and told me he and his new wife were flying to Italy for their honeymoon. New wife? How did he suddenly have a new wife? He said that they had a layover in New York, and an hour or so free at the terminal. Would I like to take the subway out to Kennedy to meet?

I rode the train to the airport, and then took the shuttle to the terminal. It was late in the day. My father, my stepmother, and I sat at a concourse bar. My father drank a martini. Maybe my stepmother had a glass of wine. Travelers and flight crews hurried past. My stepmother told me that she wanted me to think of her as a second mother. My real mother was close to dying. I told my stepmother that I would do my best. Then it was time for them to board their plane. It was a long time before I saw them again.

The paralysis of suicide is not apathy or stillness. We may feel encased, restrained somehow. Our bodies might break, or something outside us will break. What will break? We may stop opening mail, and drop contact with people. We might stop bathing or brushing our teeth, and we neither leave nor clean the house, and the dirty dishes and the dirty clothes and the week's trash and garbage might make piles that we walk around. We may feel as if we are burning, as if our cells have caught fire. We might get only a few hours of medicated sleep, or we may sleep and wake throughout the day, and that can be mistaken for resignation or apathy, but it is sickness. We picture taking the canoe out to the middle of the lake, rowing slowly over the water, and then slipping in, careful not to tip the canoe; or we pick up the pistol, the one in the cabinet, and hold it for a moment, and that helps—

the bullet will be there when we need it—and we can then place the gun back in the drawer; or we run upstairs to the roof and hang from the fire escape, but without letting go, not this time. We *are* burdens to our caretakers; we know this, no matter what you say to soothe us, no matter that you love us. If we are agitated, pacing, smoking, then we might seem to be fleeing demons, or even to be one, crazed, possessed. If we are alone in the house, we may become desperate. We watch television, into the night. Or we turn out the lights and sit, as if waiting. Is this the paralysis that we feel when threatened with violence or death? Is this our so-called fight-or-flight response? Tomorrow we will walk alone to the lake, or pull the trigger, or drop from the roof.

Why did he do it? Why did she? Why did they? What didn't we see? Is it our fault? What more could we have done? We ask ourselves versions of these questions again and again. Was it the pain? Was she unable to bear the pain? Had he become exhausted with life, and did he finally give in to despair? Wasn't she always unstable, oversensitive, crazy? Does it run in the family? Is suicide hereditary? Is it genetic? Was there a note?

One day in August, I took a walk with Nurse D. It was dinnertime. The sun was in the west, and the hallway to the dining room was bright with light from the windows facing the Hudson. I'd had five weeks of ECT. I felt stable on my feet, and felt easier talking. I asked Nurse D whether she had noticed anything—anything about me that might be different. She said that she had seen changes, they all had. The changes were audible in my voice, and I looked more relaxed. She told me that the doctors and nurses see health before the patient feels it.

"You *see?*"

Nurse D told me that I was getting well. It happens over time. The muscles in my neck and face loosened and relaxed, and my breathing got easier. I took steady breaths. My voice grew deeper, and I wasn't clumsy, only nicely depleted from treatment. I realized that I had not destroyed my life by writing about my mother. My life was not done. I could stand straight when I walked down the halls, and visitors and friends on the phone told me that I sounded better. People could stand to listen to me! The decline in psychotic certainty can be heard as the opening of new frequencies in the voice, an indication of reduced muscular tension in the chest and the face. I went to a cooking class—it was a Friday—and picked up implements, and held them, and contributed. We made hamburgers.

In the evenings, after we'd had our meds and sat beside each other on the couch, Dawn and I strolled down the hall to our bedrooms. We walked through the open doorway to the dorms, and stopped in front of her room.

Dawn had a roommate named Charlotte. We were all friends. I wished Dawn and Charlotte good sleep and sweet dreams, and hoped that they'd feel better soon. I felt safe with Dawn, safer than I'd felt at any time at the Institute. I cared so much about her and the other patients—I mean that I liked them, and felt for all of us.

We describe feeling in touch. We say that we feel in touch with the world, with people, with our feelings. Was I in touch? The daylight through the common-room windows seemed clear, somehow gentle. The sky was deep blue, going orange in the west, and the trees along the Hudson looked bright with color. I no longer minded the sound of the television. My friend Jon brought me a tiny music player, something that fit in my pocket, and Nurse D let me keep it, and I walked the halls, listening to the beat, grooving, tuned in and in touch, greeting people, chatting. My weight went up and up from the medications, and I could barely get my pants on, but I didn't care. I was alive; it was mid-August; I'd been in the hospital almost four months; I did not feel burning in my gut; my legs didn't tingle or shake; and I no longer woke in terror at three in the morning. Maybe I hadn't ruined my life, and would not spend it in institutions. Dr. A congratulated me on my recovery, on working hard and persevering. We were standing in the hallway beside the nurses' desk. He wore his white coat, and a yellow shirt with a tie. I told him that I'd had nothing to do with it, that he and his team had got me better, but he objected, repeating his praise. A day or two later, he invited me for coffee and a Danish. He unlocked the big steel door, and we left the ward. I felt uncertain at first. My doctor and I walked down the hall to the commissary. I looked out the window at the day. I felt free, not from the hospital, not from illness, just free. It felt good to be in the commissary, away from the ward, holding a cup.

I never wanted to die. Have you wanted to die? Do you now? At what stage in sickness do these desires come? Are they even desires? We might say that we are ruminating, death-obsessed, consumed. We may refer to our obsessions as intrusive thoughts, or as ideations, as if we are having *ideas* about dying, when in fact we have certainties. When were you first aware of your own death? Would you feel relieved to leave people and the world? Were you afraid that they would never understand your dying? When did you first picture your death? Can you name the day, the hour? What did you see?

My pictures began in the winter, in the months before hospitalizing. I was lying in bed. Regan slept beside me. I was sweating, and the sheets smelled like cigarettes. I went to the living room and turned on a light. It was better to sit in the light than to lie in darkness. I couldn't bear music, and movies and television shows, even comedies, scared me. I sat shivering, waiting for the sun to rise, the time when I could take another Klonopin. Why was I thinking about knives? Why couldn't I stop? Surely it would pass. I stayed quiet about it, though. Death is our burden and our comfort. No one can know.

If they know, they will worry or be scared, or threaten us with the hospital. They'll tell us that life is good; that we have only one, and that it is worth living. It is not right to die this way.

Try not to lose hope, they say. Try to stay optimistic. Keep faith. Losing us, they say, will be the end for them.

But hope to the suicide is a death sentence. The suicide cannot feel or live on hope. Our hope is gone.

I went home from the Institute by myself. I'd been there almost four months. It seemed much longer than that, though. Regan wanted me to go away with her after discharge. She said that she wanted to go somewhere quiet. I think that she wanted to celebrate, if that's the right word, my recovery. But I didn't think that I could do it. "I'm not strong enough," I told Regan, and I wasn't. Life in the world—what would that be like? What if I couldn't make it? Would I need to come back to the hospital? Would Regan and I get along? Would we have peace? Would I be a disappointment? I thought of my own quiet place, my apartment. Regan had helped me, but I felt at risk. I was afraid to resume life as it had been before the hospital.

On my last day at the Institute, the community gathered to say goodbye, a hospital tradition. Right before one of us left, the patients and the doctors and nurses gathered in the common room. I was grateful for them, for the hospital, a wondrous place. I felt gratitude, and something that seemed brand new in my life, a sense of calm, even happiness. I wished John well with his ECT, and told Helen that I saw her improving. I promised Dawn that I would stay in touch, which I did, for a while, after she got home. I shook my doctor's hand, and hugged Nurse D and the other nurses, and then I packed my clothes into my black canvas bag, and Nurse D gave me my prescriptions, my phone, and my keys. She opened the door, the gate, the portal, and I went out. The door closed, and I heard the key in the lock. I walked to the elevators, rode up a floor, and crossed the skywalk to Columbia Presbyterian, where, back in May, I'd spent the weekend in the psych emergency room, guarded by cops. There were cars on the street outside. I got in one and said hello to the driver. I rolled down the window and felt the fresh air. We drove down Riverside Drive, and then cut over to the West Side Highway. It was about four o'clock in the afternoon. To the right was the Hudson, shining in the light, and to the left were the buildings of Harlem, and then the glass and steel skyscrapers of midtown. We passed Chelsea and the Village. At Canal Street, we turned left off the highway and headed east through Chinatown to the Manhattan Bridge. We crossed the bridge and drove up Flatbush Avenue, and then turned right, and then left onto my street.

The car stopped in front of my building. I'd taken myself to the hospital in the spring, and now it was almost the end of summer. I got out of the car and stood on the sidewalk. People were out, and I could hear children playing. Had you seen me walking up the stoop, opening the front door, you might have thought that I was coming home from a job in the city or an errand in the neighborhood. I'd been gone so long, though it seemed only hours or a day.

We might recall about a period of tedium or distress that it seemed to last an eternity. Dying in psychosis, in isolation from others, takes place in a kind of eternity, though not in the same way as, say, waiting on the platform for a train running late; that eternity is a hyperbolic figure of speech. The eternity of suicide is more like the eternity that we find in myth and theology, a true forever. Our lives begin and end, friendships flourish and fail, and cultures and societies rise and fall, but, for the patient sick with suicide, history might not seem to exist.

Suicide is absolute, as is death. Ambivalence, our ability to hold many ideas and beliefs at once, is absent in the psychosis. Up on the roof, I let go of the fire escape railing and felt myself falling. Then, quickly, I caught hold. As kids, we played a game called chicken. Lying down on the road on a dark night, waiting still as the car zooms toward you, and then leaping away at the last moment, at the instant when the driver sees you lying like a corpse in the headlights, is playing chicken.

Peter and I played chicken. Peter was my friend after my family left Charlottesville for the countryside west of town. We lived at the foot of Afton Mountain, in a farmhouse that we rented. A creek ran in front of the house, and my father grew a garden out back. The garden had rows of corn and tomatoes and cucumbers and squash. I was in charge of lettuce. We had pickle barrels in the kitchen. Terry and I went to Greenwood Elementary for her fifth and my sixth grades, and then I went to Henley Junior High for seventh. Peter's father taught biology at the university, and his family hiked and camped. We camped too, but comfortably, in the Shenandoah National Park campgrounds, where my parents sat in lawn chairs and drank. I had a fantasy of hiking on the Appalachian Trail, which follows the Appalachian chain from Georgia to Maine. The trail passed a mile or two from our farm. When could we go? I begged my father. Could

Peter come? My father agreed to the trip, and we drove over the mountain to the hardware store in Waynesboro. We got backpacks, rain ponchos, freeze-dried soups and stews, and stiff, heavy boots. We planned a three-day journey, starting near the intersection of Route 250 and the Skyline Drive, which follows the mountaintops from Virginia to North Carolina. When the day came, we got up early and packed my father's black Volkswagen Beetle. We picked up Peter, drove up the mountain, and parked at a scenic overlook. There was the trail access. We got our gear and went in a line, Peter in front. My feet blistered after two hours of slipping up and down rocks and inclines, and we stopped, and I pulled off my boots and rubbed my feet. I felt embarrassed, and Peter was impatient. It was still early in the morning. This wasn't how Peter's family took a hike. They walked twenty miles in a day. We made it a couple, and then came to a place where the trail crossed the Skyline Drive again. My father told Peter and me to wait while he hitchhiked back to the Volkswagen. There was something at home that he'd forgotten to do, he said.

Peter and I sat on the side of the road, watching cars go by. Twenty minutes later, my father picked us up, and we drove down the mountain to the farm, where he opened the mail, made a phone call, put food and ice from the refrigerator in a cooler chest, and put the chest in the car.

When I told my therapist, D, this story, he suggested that my father needed a drink. Maybe that's right. We drove back up the mountain, but didn't do much hiking. Instead, we traveled in the car. We parked on the drive, and then walked to trail cabins, open, wood-framed shelters where we slept on wooden bunks and gazed up at a roof. I heard years later that Peter was dead. He crashed his car into a tree, driving home late one night from a party.

I wasn't playing chicken on the fire escape. I might or might not catch the railing before falling, might or might not fall. I did not imagine bounding from the roof in a swan dive onto the concrete, any more than I'd considered jumping from one of my apartment windows. Suicide did not seem like a choice to me, but an eternal state, like the eternity of death.

I was not aware of time, that Friday on the roof, only of screeching sounds and the helicopter overhead and my blistered hands and the cold. The sun was bright, and then the sky in the west was orange; the day got dark, and the temperature dropped, but was time speeding or slowing? We talk about the weight of the world. After ECT, the feeling in my body of immense weight went away; I felt a kind of physical lightness. I no longer required Ativan. I'd believed that I was fatal to others, and that I would be destroyed by my losses. After shocks and convulsions, after months of waiting to get well, I regained my sense of time passing. These days, I think of ECT as clean power, good electricity added to a wet, saline medium in which electrical signaling has become chaotic and mistimed.

I slept ten or eleven hours a night. I was no longer afraid to be alone in my apartment. I liked it. During the days, I went on walkabouts, exploratory expeditions up and down and across Brooklyn and Manhattan. It was summertime, and then fall, and people were out. I was not in isolation. I had solitude and contemplation, not rumination, and the world seemed to be filled with light. I told a friend that I could see the light glowing behind the leaves of the trees. Honking car horns didn't bother me. I cut my hair, and shopped for clothes that fit. My medications caused my vision to blur, and, though I wasn't reading, or not much, I began wearing reading glasses. I already had my regular pair, and so you might have seen me wearing two, one pair to look through, and the other, perched on my head, to switch to. My friend Jane had a brother who wore his glasses this way. He was schizophrenic, and lived most of his life in a private institution outside Washington, DC. Sometimes he escaped and walked around the town. Everyone knew the crazy guy with the glasses. I think that I would have liked him.

One morning in the hospital, near the end of my stay, a nurse came to my room. It was dark out, too early to be up. The nurse told me that I had a phone call. She took me down the dormitory hall. She told me that it was against the rules to wake patients for calls, but that the phone had rung and rung. It was Christa. I'd met Christa at around the same time that Regan and I remet, in the summer of 2005. She was an artist and a writer. She lived in another state. She was married, and had a sister named Cara.

Christa was crying into the phone. She told me that Cara had died. Cara had been at their mother's house. She'd shot heroin cut with fentanyl. Christa and Cara's mother found her. I stayed on the phone with Christa until the sun came up. Later that week, she drove down from New England and came to the hospital. She'd been taking anti-anxiety medication. She told me that she didn't know how she would keep living.

Immediately after leaving the hospital, I went into Dr. T's care. Once a week, I rode the subway from Brooklyn to the Upper West Side, got out at 86th Street and Central Park West, and slogged uptown. There was a food cart parked along the way, serving coffee and donuts. Typically, I bought coffee on the way to the office, and a donut on my way home. I was hungry for carbohydrates and sugar, and I was gaining more weight. My face had become round, and I had to push myself up from chairs. It didn't seem to matter how much I hiked around the city. I needed pants three sizes larger than any I'd worn before, and my shirts felt like wrappers.

I went to department stores to look at nice clothes. I wanted to feel good. I wanted to look good. I wanted to be part of things. I ate dinner by myself at a local bar, and searched for books in secondhand bookstores, books that I might want to read one day, or that might be useful to me when I began writing again. But I had no clear idea what that meant—writing again. It didn't matter. Someday I would, I supposed, write, the way I once had.

I sat out on benches and watched people walk by. After some time went by, and I felt more confident, I made plans and met people for dinner. I rode the subway. I felt good, but the time of suicide was close, recent, and several times I had the feeling that I was falling back, as it were, slipping. I felt that I was losing my balance. My heart raced, and the crushing feeling returned. Dr. T told me that this could happen, that I might get tremors, aftershocks, as it were, but that they would go away.

Regan and I saw each other, though less over the months. I stayed in my apartment, and Regan stayed in hers. Regan had taken care of me, and hoped, I think, that my wellness would lead to good changes in me, and therefore between us. But I didn't know what I was supposed to do or be. During the months following ECT, I felt calm and at peace, but also that I was vulnerable.

I couldn't, at that time, describe my homecoming, but now I can say, speaking poetically, that I felt naked. My face in the bathroom mirror was my face, no longer disfigured. My apartment was the same apartment, on the same block. The houses were the same as before, and so were the trees outside the living room window. I saw people walking their dogs or pushing children in strollers or coming home from work. I slept in my own bed, and made coffee in the morning. I didn't make many plans. And I didn't cook much at first, though eventually I did. I was capable. I could use utensils. In the hospital, I'd been certain that my life had been defined by errors and mistakes, but now I was not so sure. I felt that I'd been through something, jumped a gorge, as it were, died and come back. I might have told you that I'd had a breakdown. But that word seems misleading to me now. What, after all, is breaking? Are we made of parts that break?

That fall and winter and spring, I kept Regan at a distance, and made excuses. She lived only ten minutes away. I became afraid to go see her. I did not feel as I had at any time before, not a year or two earlier, or five or ten, or when I was younger, back at school. I'd lost my mother. My mother was gone. I couldn't imagine life or a future, but I was free of symptoms, free of suicide. I was no longer psychotic. Reconnecting with people, or making new connections, seemed important, but I wasn't in a hurry. I slept for months, it seems now. I slept and slept, through the fall and winter and into spring. I hadn't been able to sleep at all, and now sleep came on hard; it was imperturbable, and I woke feeling safe, not startled, not panicked. I changed the sheets, vacuumed the floors, washed the dishes, and kept the bathroom clean. I trimmed my beard and tucked in my shirt.

Most of what we say about suicide has nothing to do with suicide. Breakdown is not an accurate word for suicide, any more than it would be for tuberculosis or cancer. Depression is another misleading term, as are madness, lunacy, hysteria, the blues, despair, and so on— all words that speak to appearances, or to the affect and the disorganized behavior of the patient. But the patient dying of suicide need not seem mad or lunatic or despairing. We most likely do not necessarily appear to be "out of our minds."

The terms that we use to describe illness can either inform or impede our understanding. We can speak and write in language that expresses tactility and touch, not theory and abstraction. We can figure forth meaning in appearances, or we can question appearances. To say, for instance, that suicides are naturally impulsive people is to miss the hours, months, and years of anxiety and physical deterioration, the fear and the seeming resignation with which we go to our deaths. Or we might think the catatonic torpid, and not understand the anguish, the feeling of the body somehow vibrating, the paralysis. The man on the bridge may spend hours perched at the railing, peering down, afraid to look. The woman in the waves does not splash her way into the sea, but more likely walks slowly, until she is submerged. We think of gun suicides as violent, rather than merciful. Better to say that suicides are sick and at risk, rather than needy, disturbed, or crazy. Suicide is not a storm or a conflagration, a deluge or an inferno.

Each era sees the world in terms of its own technologies. Friends and lovers are on the same frequency, accident victims go into shock, the successful enjoy power, and frustration might cause you to blow a fuse. Our current imagery for suicide is not possible without computers and an electrical grid. We imagine our brains and bodies as wired, and when we are tired we might say that we are off-line, or powered down, or that we need a reboot. Are we on the same wavelength? Freud, who posits an unruly id, a willful ego, and a controlling superego as a system, and who writes about pressures, drives, and releases, invokes the coal furnaces, steam engines, and valves and stoppers of the Industrial Revolution. Paracelsus, the sixteenth-century itinerant Swiss doctor who discovered and named miners' disease, black lung, writes about illness in alchemical terms. Paracelsus might speak of the moon and the stars, and then prescribe mineral and vegetable tinctures and compounds. We still use pharmaceutical compounds, which we call psychiatric medications. Hippocrates, writing around 450–400 BC, centuries before dissection and the study of anatomy and pathology became medical practice, describes delirium and convulsions in naturalistic terms. About epilepsy, then popularly taken as a form of divine possession, he writes, "This so-called 'sacred disease,' is due to the same causes as all other diseases, to the things we see come and go, the cold and the sun too, the changing and inconstant winds." Hippocrates looks to nature, to the body, to what we can see, hear, touch, and feel, the things in the world that we can concretely describe.

All our diseases are terrifying until they are known and named. A good example is consumption, which we could call a historical disease. Consumption was marked by coughing, weakness, night sweats, pallor, fevers, weight loss, difficulty breathing, bloody sputum, and the visible collapse of the patient's chest, a kind of drying and shrinking of the body, as if the patient were being consumed, eaten away from within. Hippocrates knew the disease as *phthisis*—the wasting disease—and over the centuries it has had other names, among them the "white death," an allusion to the pale, wasted look of the sufferer. In the sixteenth century, doctors suggested that contagion might be the route for infection, rather than God, heredity, alchemical misalignments, or problems with the patient's traits and dispositions. You could be seen as the consumptive type, prone to tragic, early death. In the late eighteenth and early nineteenth centuries, consumptive emaciation became associated with beauty. Emily and Anne Brontë both died of consumption. Chopin and Chekhov were consumptives. In the nineteenth century, the removal of the sick to mountain retreats became the main treatment in Europe and America. Patients rested in bed or reclined in chairs set out in the fresh air. Then, in 1882, a Berlin physician named Robert Koch isolated a bacillus, Mycobacterium tuberculosis, as the cause, and the name "consumption" has since fallen from use. The disease is no longer a romance; it has lost its mystique. We refer to tuberculosis now, and treat it with antibiotics.

In the late summer of 2008, David Foster Wallace died. He hanged himself. I found out at my fiftieth birthday party. Christa threw the party at my friend Jon's apartment on the Upper East Side. Many of the people who'd visited me at the Psychiatric Institute were there, other writers, people I worked with. I thanked them for helping me survive. Then, after most everyone had left, Jon told me about David. I felt that I'd lost a comrade in survival. He'd died on September 12, my mother's birthday. Jon asked me if I would be all right.

Wallace was a famous writer—or we should say that he is one. He was, and is, regarded as a literary genius. His death was celebrated in magazines, and a movie about his life appeared. He'd written novels and stories that are built from his own experience of suicide, and after his death, that writing took on the dual qualities of prophecy and evidence, as if David's death established his authenticity and value, his worth to us. The death by suicide of the public figure is invariably controversial, and we interpret it widely. In David's case, as is true with many artists who die this way, the news was shocking—and then not. We speak of the pain of the creative process, of loneliness, invention, and the fear of the blank page. What torment *drives* the artist? What makes a writer? What is genius? Might fame be linked with suicide? But these are old questions.

If you've said that you are well when you're in danger, then you may know the feeling that you are, as it were, hoarding death. Maybe we aren't lying when we deny our condition and the danger—not exactly. Our smiles are forced and our voices are flat. We tell others not to worry. But are we simply powerless to say otherwise? People remark, about a drunk's abusive style, "That's the booze talking," and though booze doesn't talk, we take the meaning. Our claims of wellness, our promises that we will never succumb, are a little like the booze talking.

Is it logical to imagine that psychotic self-evaluations are cogent? The notion that we choose death over pain, fundamental to our current thinking on suicide, suggests that we choose at all, as if some part of us exists outside the illness, unaffected, taking in the situation and making rational decisions. A fickle person might say, on some Saturday night, "Part of me wants to go to the party, but part of me wants to stay home." What are these parts, and where are they to be found? When I was sick in the hospital, there was no deciding on much besides how best to lie on the sofa, which side of my body to rest on, how to tuck and arrange the black canvas bag against the sofa arm, and whether to face the light or turn inward and press my face against the cushion. Asking for extra meds was never a decision or a choice. It was something that I did in order to stop shaking, to feel a little safe. I curled up or stretched out on the common-room sofa, but in every position, I felt panic. Where could I run? Where was I safe? I was trapped in the wrong hospital, I thought, but I took my meds, and waited and waited. I waited for nortriptyline to work, and after that I waited for ECT to work. I waited for dinner or fresh air or a minute of sleep. When I came too quickly toward my doctor, when, that day at the Institute nurses' station, I charged forward and demanded that I be moved to another hospital, I was really only trying to talk to him, wasn't I?

They drank and drank, my mom and dad. They drank through the night. I can see them, sitting in chairs with their cigarettes piling up in ashtrays beside them. She's in the living room. He's in the kitchen, pouring another martini. It's late. The house is filled with cigarette smoke. The lights are out. My mother has been howling, screaming. Now she has her legs stretched out on an ottoman. Her toes curl and straighten, curl and straighten; it's a tic. Soon she will pass out, but not yet. She has more cigarettes. She has more condemnations for my father, and even for me. "You can have a say around here when you pay rent!" she shouts. I am thirteen, fourteen, fifteen. She inhales from her cigarette. It flares, briefly lighting her face. She is haggard and gray. Her hair is wild. Her speech is slurry and hard to understand. She calls my father a motherfucker and a shit. She has at him for his affairs. He rarely defends himself. He laughs her off, goes to the kitchen, and opens the freezer for more gin. He tells Terry and me that our mother is just tired. "She needs rest," he says. "She works so hard." Our mother never struck my sister, but she struck me. On a very bad night, she might charge into my room with her arm raised. There were no hugs in our family; no hello or goodbye kisses on the cheek. I never saw my father put his arm around my mother's shoulders or her waist.

He gave her nice things for Christmas, but it infuriated her, as it might you or me.

Vocal constriction may be a symptom of suicidal illness. We all know the worrisome sound of the sick. The suicide's distress may be audible. We might shriek. As heart and pulmonary distress increase, our fear may grow constant, and our posture droops, but we're not merely lazy or weak; we feel that we are under a crushing weight—we *can't* stand straight, except through exertion. Our muscles may tremble, and our joints might become inflamed. We may become short of breath. We don't yawn, or we yawn all the time. But our fatigue is nothing like the tiredness that follows a busy day. When we panic, our hearts beat faster and then faster, until we are gasping. We feel cold, and may even evacuate our bowels. Our bodies might be saturated with adrenalin and cortisol, two hormones associated with the fight-or-flight response. Confronted with a threat, do we run or do we defend ourselves? In deep illness, we can neither fight nor flee. We are not facing a wild animal or an assaulter. But there is nonetheless great threat. Maybe the threat will come in the mailbox, or on a phone call, or during a meeting or an appointment, some terrifying outing. The threat might be a car backfiring, or a view from a height, or other people, and so we don't step outside the house, or leave our bedrooms, or pick up the phone.

The illness itself is the threat. We might pace or sit motionless, afraid to move, unable to move. Don't touch me, we might say. Are we playing dead? Are we paralyzed with everlasting fear? When I was sick, I felt that my body was poisoned and poisonous, and I felt that this poison had invaded every cell. I felt the poison as aching and burning. I couldn't change my thoughts or lessen my pain. I believed that I saw the world and my situation clearly, that my thinking was good. Lying on the living room floor, on the tarp, with the knife and the pills, I had the sense that I was drying out, collapsing from within. I felt poisoned in my gut and my brain, and on the surface of my skin.

What is psychotic rumination? We may say that we are spinning and spiraling. Or that we are cycling, or in a loop; our thoughts, we say, are intrusive, inescapable— bad imaginings that we try and try again not to have, to *see*. Or can rumination be imagined as something concrete and organic, like alcoholic perseveration, the drunk's fixations and repetitions? Whatever they seem to be *about*, are suicidal ruminations *ideas* about dying, or do they describe a natural history, straightforward symptoms of a fatal disease that requires the hand? Does the suicide have ideas about death, or might the ideation in fact belong to all of us, to you and me, society's collective fears and beliefs about suicide and the sick individual? Why do people "kill themselves?" we wonder, grammatically imparting will in dying. My drunk father said about my drunk mother, "She's tired, she's tired," and then insisted on his love for my sister and me, after which he sat into the night in his underwear, weeping in the dark. Alcoholics repeat themselves, say the same irrational things over and over, but we do not call alcoholic perseveration intrusive thought or ideation. We politely say that alcoholics like to drink, or that they drink too much, or that they should stop. In the nineteenth and early twentieth century, before AA, during the temperance movement, alcoholism and its effects on the body and society were blamed on temptation, preference, and irreligion, not addiction. No alcoholic ever got sober from shame, and no suicide gets well from prejudice or pity.

After I left the hospital, friends joked that I was crazy, and I laughed along. Some suggested that a psychiatric history might enhance my literary reputation. Had you met me then, I might have cracked that I'd had "a lot of ECT," in order to make comedy of my difficulty finding words or remembering names, as if it were my responsibility to make others comfortable with my new disability. I was thirty pounds heavier, and then more. I haunted department stores, getting to know imported brands that I sometimes bought on sale, wool and silk to hide my

body. My mother was a textile artist and fashion conser-
vator. She'd studied tailoring in the 1950s, and built a suit
for my father in the seventies. Years later, in the nineties, she promised to make me one, but I guess we forgot
about it. I felt communion with her on the sales floors,
pulling hangers off racks and putting them back.

Once every month or so, Christa drove to Brooklyn.
Sometimes she told me that she wanted to marry me.
She promised that she'd be a good partner. She wanted
children. She was underweight, had circles around her
eyes, and cried over the loss of her sister. She came up
the stairs breathless from the climb. It was the spring
of 2007, and then summer. Little by little, we began a
relationship. I cooked for her, and she told stories of her
divorce. We drove around in her car, and had picnics in
the park. Was she in danger of suicide? Caretaking was
reassuring to me. When I'd been sick, I'd been afraid of
poverty, sure of it coming, but it turned out that there
was enough in the bank to last awhile, money from *The
Afterlife*, and for an unfinished novel that seemed, after
everything that had happened, irrelevant. The novel
concerned a family living on a hilltop in the south,
someplace resembling the Blue Ridge Mountains in
Virginia. The father is an autodidact T. S. Eliot scholar,
and, in a basement workshop full of leather and lasts,
makes special shoes for the mother. The shoes are too

tight. They're made that way on purpose. The shoes are designed to make the mother stop drinking. Upstairs, the sister lies in a bed covered with stuffed animals. She breathes through an oxygen tank. A sorceress with a magic parsnip lives in a trailer on the mountainside; and a veterinary doctor treats the narrator for his problems of living. That's about as far as I got. Was writing over? I didn't try for a long time.

Psychotic people almost always disavow suicide, believing without ambivalence in the need for secrecy. We may believe that our worldview is the correct one. We do this even when we are close to dying. We do this in horrible pain. Is suicide our refuge? I couldn't imagine, sitting before the doctors in the Institute dining room, that day in the summer of 2006, that I was psychotic, even though I'd nearly dropped from the fire escape, and had been in anguish in the hospital, and had seen my face disfigured in the bathroom mirror. "You're psychotic," the head ECT doctor told me, that morning in the ward dining room. She said, "You're sick," and I cried that I wasn't, not in the way she meant. It was only that I'd ruined everything, would lose everyone, no matter what she said, or what the others holding clipboards scribbled down. I was crying, and then wailing. The tears ran down my face. I'd been condemned, and would be branded, marked deficient, and discarded by everyone, friends and colleagues and the people I might one day meet.

Those fears and certainties were with me a long time before I got so sick, though only intermittently and less floridly. They'd been my fears since I was a child, and they have shaped my life. To the sick, fears are perceptions of reality. There is discrimination that we see, or should see, like unequal salaries for women and people of color, and there is discrimination that we don't see. We might not immediately feel the wariness of others, or notice the slow dwindling of invitations and social opportunities, or understand the denial of promotions at work. Groups that suffer discrimination, ethnic minorities, people of color, and persecuted religious congregations, can nonetheless make communities and traditions, however dangerous this might be. Coherent bonding is difficult for those of us who "lose our minds." For us, the loss of community is a symptom of an illness that only grows as personal isolation intensifies. After I left the hospital, people looked at me with skepticism, and stood at a slight angle, as if objectively appraising me. In conversations, my partners leaned backward rather than forward. Was it safe? Was I safe? Maybe my friends were worried that I'd flip out. Small talk was an ordeal. Misunderstandings were common. There was the time when I was on the phone to an old friend, Jo, in New

Hampshire. "That makes me want to jump out the window," I said about something or other. It was a provocative remark, but not a threat. But how was my friend to know this? I said, "That makes me want to jump out the window," and then my phone battery died, and a short while later, two police cars screeched up the street. I heard their car doors slamming. I was in my underwear. The buzzer rang, and I pulled on my pants and let in the cops, who charged up the stairs and banged on the apartment door. "Hang on, I'm getting dressed," I shouted. My pants were unbuttoned. There were four policemen. They came into the apartment. I buttoned my pants, got my phone and my keys, and then the police handcuffed and walked me down the stairs. A policeman put his hand on my head and eased me into the back seat of his squad car. At the hospital, another policeman unlocked my right hand from the handcuffs, and then fixed that cuff around a metal railing on the wall. I said that I was a writer, but the doctors weren't impressed. I asked if they'd tried any of the numbers on my phone. Had they called Jo? An older doctor was in and out, and younger ones, the residents, came to ask questions. I told them my history, but added that I was all right, that today had been a misunderstanding. Four hours later, I was allowed to go.

Jo was afraid to talk to me. She thought that I would

scold her. I told her that she'd done the right thing, and that the cops and the hospital had too, that no one got hurt. My friend had had reason to worry for me. She protected me. But her worry, and that of others, effectively compounded my own, as if I were being reminded that I was sick. I pretended that my life was in order, and, in 2008, went off my medications. My doctor resisted, but I told her that I felt better without the meds. And, for a while, I did. I tried riding my bike, but was awkward and unbalanced, and couldn't get up hills. I preferred sitting on benches. I wrote a story about a man in a failing marriage, who, after discovering that his bank account is empty and his credit cards canceled, runs from a florist's shop with a bouquet of stolen flowers for his alcoholic wife. What did I know about husbands and wives? It felt good to write, but the feeling didn't last. Christa came and went, and I taught workshops in writing. I told my students that each of them had stories that no one else in the world could tell. I told them that it didn't matter where they came from, or from what kind of people. I suggested that trauma informs all our writing, and told them to describe the world, so that they and their readers could *see*, and to write their characters' predicaments as realities. I told my students that their solitude in writing need not become loneliness in life. But I felt treacherous, as if my teaching would lead them into danger.

In 2009, just days before Christmas, in the Madrid airport, my father died. He and my stepmother were on their way to Venice. My father fell asleep and didn't wake up. My stepmother's voice on the phone was a scream. His head had been resting on her shoulder. She'd felt his breathing stop. It was his heart. The medics tried but failed to revive him. My stepmother was alone, and the body needed to be sent to America. I remember my father's face, his grin, and the warm and affectionate look in his eyes when he took his first drink of the night.

It's illogical to think that the suicide wants to die. We say that we do, but do we? I believe that we can reverse our thinking about the suicide's apparent desires and intentions, and follow an opposite thread; we can consider that the suicide wants to live, and begin to think more concretely, rather than scratch our heads about what causes suicide. Ruminations on dying might seem less like fantasies or wishes. Our claims of our worthlessness might be heard as disease markers rather than sentimental pleas. Do we imagine the pain in our bodies, or are our bodies, flooded with stress hormones, sleep-deprived, motor functioning failing, in a kind of toxic shock? Is rumination a form of isolation? Are our plans for dying forestallments of dying? I have a friend who saved prescription pills for two years. She lived in Greenwich Village, on a high floor of a large apartment building. Her father had raped her when she was two. She never thought of the window, and never swallowed the pills. She told me that collecting them comforted her. She is alive now.

Was my friend trying to die? Have you tried to die? Have you found how difficult it is? Maybe you've stayed alive for months, or years, and gone to therapists, and tried medications. Maybe you've been in a hospital already, maybe more than once; maybe you admit and discharge, admit and discharge. Your friends know the sound of your voice when you're not well, and ask if you're all right. Do you say that it's a hard day? Are there friends to tell? Do you move about the house like an invalid, not dressing or picking things up off the floor, not eating or reading the mail? Do you sit without moving, your muscles tight? Is this fight-or-flight, or is it a fear that we feel more deeply than that, older in our history, the anxiety not of the threatened animal but of the dying animal? Helplessness is perpetual for the suicide, a chronic condition, and makes a new sort of everyday life.

For the suicide, these are material concerns, not musings. In late 2010, Christa told me that she had met another man. It was sudden news, and winter was coming. Soon it would be Christmas. My father had been dead a year. I was in grief, and then terror. Almost immediately, the symptoms that I had felt in the spring of 2006 returned. I lay in bed at night, awake in the dark, scared of the dark. I felt my heart pounding. I couldn't eat. Every night, I was afraid of going to bed. I took Ativan. I stopped sleeping. Dying felt close again. The pressure in my chest returned. I felt that my anxiety had somehow moved to a place deep in my body, had become a hum, a vibration. I walked around the city without knowing where I was. This happened in places with which I was familiar. It happened in my own neighborhood. Sometimes, I had to look up at the street signs, and then ponder over the direction that I should take to get home. I rode in cabs, and came upstairs to my apartment and sat and trembled. After a month of this, I told Dr. T that I needed to hospitalize again. Dr. T wanted to know whether I was having a fantasy of care, a desire for someone to watch over me. Did I really need the hospital again? I told her that I must admit, that I knew this from the symptoms that I was feeling, so like those that I'd felt before. She arranged for a bed. I called a car and rode up the West Side Highway, just as I had in 2006. The Hudson was to the left, and the city to the right.

It was November. I thought that I might have ECT and then go home. Instead, I spent another four-month period as a patient, first at Columbia Presbyterian, and then back at the Institute. But it wasn't like before. I had thirty-seven rounds. There was no euphoria this time, no steady improvement, no turnaround. I lay on the operating table, weeping over Christa. I urged my fellow patients toward ECT, and then watched them go home. I thought about sharp objects, and pictured myself bleeding, or hanging from a knotted sheet. The nurses kept me company on walks through the halls, like in the old days. I asked them who would ever want me. Who could accept me? "Look at me," I said. I begged for reassurances, and they told me that I was loved, and that people needed me to survive and live a good life, and that the doctors would never give up. I would get better, they said. At night, before my medicated sleep, I read the poems of Robert Lowell, who writes of his own times in psychiatric hospitals.

But I left the hospital unwell. The compression in my chest had lessened, and my anxiety no longer felt as if it originated in my muscles and bones. Just the same, I was anxious, and back on lithium and nortriptyline. It was spring 2011, and then summer, five years since the first hospitalization. I was afraid that I wouldn't make it, wouldn't be able to live and sustain myself. But I also remembered feeling healthy. That summer, I began a relationship with Cynthia, who worked for a city agency and carried a badge. Cynthia and I had mutual friends. She had a Bernese mountain dog named Rose. We called her the Bear, and invented an imaginary world in which the Bear was a great scientist, hard at work, whenever Cynthia and I were out of the house, on absurd solutions to the world's problems. Cynthia told me that the Bear would help me, and she was right. I walked the Bear, and we had petting sessions. I scratched her ears. Cynthia said, "Where's your belly?" and the Bear rolled onto her back with her paws in the air. At night, the Bear watched over us. She slept by the door, and then, later in the night, in the hall; and in the morning we found her beside the bed. She died in 2015. She'd lived a good, long life. She had cancer and dysplasia; she couldn't easily move her hind legs, or balance herself. She spent the days lying on the floor. On the last morning of her life, though, before the vet came to euthanize her, she got up. She stood by herself, and walked to the bathroom. Cynthia and I bathed her. We toweled her dry, and later our friends who knew the Bear came to say goodbye. It was a Friday. The day was cold, and the light outside the windows was fading. Cynthia, the doctor, and I sat in a circle on the floor. The Bear rested her head in Cynthia's lap, and I put my hand on the Bear's side. The vet pushed in the needle, and I felt the Bear's breathing stop.

My family is gone now, all but Terry, her husband, John, and their two children, Tim and Liz. They live across the country. My sister and I don't talk much these days, not since we lost our parents, not since I got so sick. In the year after the Bear died, Cynthia and I parted.

What is suicide? Why do we have it? We talk about the brain and the mind. One is an organ, and the other seems a mystery. Deprived of touch, our bodies and our brains might suffer, as does our capacity for social life. We may seem "mindless" or "crazy" or "mad," or we might appear sullen, or rebellious; or we cry and cry, or never cry, or overeat, or starve ourselves; we tremble, and yell at our partners and siblings, and carry out our own violence. Some victims of trauma learn to seek and perpetrate abuse. Abuse at a young age affects development. The effects last through life. Trauma can cause changes in our brains and our bodies. Must we distinguish between brain and body? Can we say whether our brains control our bodies, or whether our bodies inform our brains? Does my heart pound in anxiety, or am I anxious because my heart is pounding? Am I out of breath because I'm scared, or am I feeling scared because I am in cardiac and pulmonary distress? Am I better off dead, or do I feel the urgent need to warn you about a crisis that can kill you? Does my psychosis originate in areas of my brain, or is psychotic rumination an expectable expression of a more global sickness? Am I untouchable because I am sick, or am I sick because I am not touched?

My hands got stiff. I was cold. My joints hurt. Tingling pain spread up my legs. My voice was flat. The light hurt my eyes. Sounds were irritants. My breathing became shallow and effortful. My skin broke out. I could not get an erection. I had hypertension and tachycardia. I couldn't smile, laugh, or stand straight. I lost my appetite and weight, and hid in my apartment, and crossed my arms over my chest. I lost all feeling of safety and security. I curled in a ball. I saw myself broken on the patio beneath the fire escape. I had the feeling sometimes that people, even my close friends, were poking at me, poking and retreating, as if checking to see whether I was dead enough to leave behind. My illness was not confined to my brain or my body. Even after I'd got out of the hospital, it troubled everyone around me. Stigma is not merely a social imposition of hatred. It is not unilateral. I accommodated my own shunning. I stopped answering the phone. I stopped seeing people. I turned the lock. It was shame. Up on the roof, that Friday in 2006, I imagined my life reduced, compromised, evacuated of people, but I'd not imagined my own hand in achieving this. I'd not seen, then, how I would retreat, never feeling welcome or wanted. Are you ashamed of your life? Are you afraid that people will know something about you? What will they know? Will you be picked for the interview, for the promotion, for your hand in marriage?

The term "mind" need not refer to a concept. I understand mind as empathy, which we wrongly equate with compassion and kindness. I think of empathy as an awareness of others, not as a category of feeling or gestures. The seventeenth-century philosopher René Descartes writes, "I think, therefore I am," giving rise to our belief that each of us lives independently from other people. The prisoner in isolation is not independent, but in anguish. The person whose sexuality must be hidden or denied lives in isolation, not independence. Bullied children who don't leave their rooms are not seeking solitude. The homeless, many expelled from our depleted hospital system, are our Bedlam. The asylums of the nineteenth and early twentieth centuries, designed as working communities, institutional homes for people who need them, are largely gone. We walk and drive past our homeless sick and dying, and our neglect is murder. "We are born alone and we die alone," people say, as if we don't have mothers and fathers, sisters and brothers, good or bad homes, losses that we suffer. We say that we lose our minds, but what we lose may be our bonds with others. I understand mind as brain, body, and environment—your body, my body, the body politic, the body electric. Were it up to me, I might give this illness a whole new name, not depression or even suicide or psychosis. I might call suicide death in place. The name speaks to the body in sickness and in society, to a death that seems to exist everywhere and nowhere. Death in place presents with compression in the chest and the clumsiness and exhaustion that come with movement of any kind. It presents as agitation and anxiety. Can we imagine a dying process writ large, our bodies saturated with stress hormones, insufficiently oxygenated, deprived of sleep, our muscles and joints aching, our neuronal signaling and organ and gastrointestinal functioning gone awry, our faces expressionless, our hands clenched? Do we recede from others and the world in sadness, in anger, in grief? Do we have a so-called chemical imbalance, or some genetic predisposition to suicide? Do we have disorders and comorbidities? Can the problem be found in our serotonin levels, our norepinephrine, or a deficiency of dopamine? Are we short on oxytocin, the chemical associated with bonding between mother and child? Oxytocin produces feelings of warmth and attachment. In sickness, we feel neither of those things. We become rigid. We take shallow breaths. Our hearts beat and beat. We are like babies needing to be held. If we are not held, then we will not thrive. We say that our heads are heavy, and that we carry the weight of the world. The statement, "My burden is my death and your life," understood literally, could help us better cope with this disease. And Descartes, amended, might read, "I feel, therefore we are." But who would think such a thing in a society like ours, where individualism is praised and social support agencies go underfunded? Suicide seems simply to *happen*, for reasons that we believe cannot be known. And yet we blame ourselves when we lose people. Do we fail the suicide, or do we condemn the suicide?

We have the hospital. I was there. I wanted to live and not die. The hospital's floors and white walls, and the bedrooms and bathrooms, were clean. The patients were not beaten, humiliated, or shoved aside. Medication was never forced. Solitude was possible, but no one was kept in isolation. A nurse was always close. I had my black canvas bag, with nothing in it that could harm me. There was soap on the bathroom sink ledge, and coffee with breakfast, and the comfort of other patients. We need our hospitals. We aren't madmen or impulsive, wild-eyed types. We are your neighbors, your friends. We are students and singers, grandmothers and addicts. Maybe we're you. What story can you tell? How does it begin? What can you see? What can you touch and feel? You will need to describe the chair in the corner, and the cup on the table, and the window that looks out on the swing set in the backyard. Is there a path through the trees? Who lives in your part of the world? What language do they speak?

As long as we see suicide as a rational act taken after rational deliberation, it will remain incomprehensible. Stigma, society's unacknowledged violence toward the

sick, will remain strong. But if we accept that the suicide is trying to survive, then we can begin to describe
an illness. I believe that we must make this leap in our
thinking. We must rule out myth and speculation. This
letter, this report, this book, seeks a paradigm shift in our
understanding of suicide in society. It finds neither will
nor agency in suicide, only dying, and calls for a great
commitment to the hospital, to our community and our
health. What is the hospital, if not all of us? What is medicine, if not touch? Suicide must not be imagined as enig-
matic; it isn't poetry or philosophy. I have come to think
of suicide as a natural history that may begin in trauma
and abjection, or the withdrawal of touch, and that ends
in death by one's own hand. The purpose of suicide is
death, not what we may think of as rage, revenge, or
atonement for sin. To the extent that the suicide acts, it is
but a falling away.

I am married now. My wife's name is Marija. She is a
classical pianist. She is an only child. Our friends Sasha
and Vlada introduced us in late 2016. She was born in
Belgrade, Serbia, and came to New York in the early
nineties for conservatory. Back in Belgrade, she has her
aunt Zora, her mother's sister; and her cousins, Milos
and Milan; and Milos's mother, Marija's father's step-
sister, Olga. Milan is married to Tijana; and Milos and
his wife, also named Marija, have two grown daughters,

Tara and Una. Three years before she and I met, Marija
lost her mother, and her father died shortly after we met.
Her mother's name was Dušanka, and her father's was
Dragoslav; his friends called him Spika. Spika was a civil
engineer. I remember the morning in Brooklyn when
Marija got the phone call telling her that her father had
had a stroke. It was winter, 2017. Marija and I had been
together two months. She screamed and fell to the floor.

She found him in intensive care at Belgrade's main
neurology hospital, in the middle of the city. She was
allowed an hour each day with him. He couldn't speak
or move. He'd lain on the floor for six hours before
one of his employees found him. She thought that he
seemed to see her. She held his hand and told him that
she was beside him. Could he hear her? None of the
other patients seemed to be doing well. Marija went to
the hospital every day. She and I talked on the phone.
She was not sleeping. We made plans to live in Serbia
while her father recovered. Would it help him to be
in the countryside? Should he be in a private hospital?
Should he at least have his own room? He was seventy-
five. She stayed with him a month, and then he died.
I bought a ticket, packed my suitcase, called a car, and
rode to the airport.

The plane landed in Belgrade early on a Thursday.
Marija's father's funeral was the next day, Friday. The

funeral was held at an old Orthodox cemetery on a hill-side, with stone crypts rising above the ground, and walking paths that descended steeply and then wound around the hill. Marija's father's grave was next to her mother's. Her mother's was sealed; her father's was open. Avala Mountain was visible in the distance. Marija, her cousins and nieces, her aunt Zora, and I stood in a line in a small chapel, a shed, really, with stone floors and walls, and a low ceiling. The priest swung his censer, and people passed through, a procession, everyone holding candles. They passed before the family, and then, one after another, stood their candles in a metal box with a sand bottom. Here were the old friends and fellow builders and engineers, and the children of friends already dead, and classmates from school, and people who'd owed Spika money, or from whom he'd borrowed, aging businessmen and a few mafiosi from the Yugoslav years. An hour passed; the candle box seemed ablaze; its fire lit the room. And then the candles began to melt. By the time the service was over, there was only liquid wax, filling the box.

After the funeral, Marija's friends and family members clutched my hand and told me that they didn't know what would become of Marija without me. We were all meeting for the first time. I was glad that I was there. Marija and I have been together since. We married in late

2017, at city hall in Brooklyn. Couples waited in line to stand before the justice of the peace and say their vows. The people waiting seemed to come from every part of the world, and to belong to every nationality and race. It was a hectic scene.

Marija said, "I do."

"I do," I said.

Now we spend Christmas and part of the summer in Belgrade. We sometimes think of moving there. Mainly, though, and for now, we live in the apartment in Brooklyn, the apartment from which, a decade and a half ago, I ran to the roof and hung from the fire escape. I still suffer anxiety, some days, and remain vigilant over my moods, and always will. I don't always sleep well. I am sometimes fearful, though not of the hospital, which for me was medicine and asylum.

I am home with Marija. She sits at the piano, and I sit on the living room sofa, writing to you. The piano's sound is rich and full, and I can feel the vibrations through the floor and in the air. The vibrations are Chopin, or Janáček, or Bach. I vibrate too; the sensation is of hearing and feeling; electricity, therapy, harmony. At night in bed, Marija and I can see the fire escape. We see it outside the bedroom window, its dark outline against the city sky, the metal steps going up or down. I remember that Friday in April, that day on the roof, that time, that life, those friends, the months and years, that eternity. What will you remember? What will you write in your letter to a friend you can trust? And were you to write and send that letter, do you think that it could change the world?

Acknowledgments

I wish to thank the people who believed in this book before it was a book; my editor at Norton, Jill Bialosky, and her assistant, Drew Elizabeth Weitman; Rebecca Nagel, Tracy Bohan, and Andrew Wylie, my agents; and Dorothy Janick and Liping Wang; my former teachers John Reimers and Allan Gurganus; and Deborah Trcisman, my editor at *The New Yorker*, who listened to me talk about this book for countless hours, and who read scores of early pages. Dawn Skorczewski, Lewis Allen Kirshner, and Anna Ornstein introduced me to a circle of doctors in Boston, with whom I met several times.

Andrea Benzacar's suggestions brought clarity and sense. My friends Jane Shapiro and Mark Singer were invaluable company along the way. My greatest debt is to my wife, Marija, who read the manuscript and was always enthusiastic and reassuring. Writing began at the MacDowell Colony and continued at the Corporation of Yaddo. This book would not be here at all were it not for a generous fellowship grant from the John D. and Catherine T. MacArthur Foundation.

Works Consulted

Alcoholics Anonymous, *The Big Book.*

Bliss, Michael. *William Osler: A Life in Medicine.*

Bowlby, John. *Attachment.*

————. *Loss: Sadness and Depression.*

————. *A Secure Base: Parent-Child Attachment and Healthy Human Development.*

————. *Separation: Anxiety and Anger.*

Cregan, Mary. *The Scar: A Personal History of Depression and Recovery.*

de Waal, Frans. *Primates and Philosophers: How Morality Evolved.*

Dunbar, Robin. *Grooming, Gossip, and the Evolution of Language.*

Durkheim, Émile. *Suicide.*

Erikson, Erik H. *Childhood and Society.*

Freud, Sigmund. *The Standard Edition of the Complete Psychological Works.*

Goffman, Erving. *Asylums: Essays on the Social Stimulation of Mental Patients and Other Inmates*

Grevens, Phillip. *Spare the Child: The Religious Roots of Punishment and the Psychological Impact of Physical Abuse.*

Grob, Gerald N. *The Mad Among Us: A History of the Care of America's Mentally Ill.*

Herman, Judith, MD. *Trauma and Recovery: The Aftermath of Violence—From Domestic Abuse to Political Terror.*

Hyde, Lewis. *Imagination and the Erotic Life of Poetry.*

Jamison, Kay Redfield. *Night Falls Fast: Understanding Suicide.*

Lieberman, Mathew D. *Social: Why Our Brains Are Wired to Connect.*

Lloyd, G. E.R., ed. *Hippocratic Writings.*

Masson, Jeffrey Moussaieff. *The Assault on Truth: Freud's Suppression of the Seduction Theory.*

Miller, Alice. *Breaking Down the Wall of Silence: The Liberating Experience of Facing Personal Truth.*

————. *The Drama of the Gifted Child: The Search for the True Self.*

————. *For Your Own Good: Hidden Cruelty in Childhood and the Roots of Violence.*

————. *Thou Shalt Not Be Aware: Society's Betrayal of the Child.*

Mitchell, Stephen A., and Margaret J. Black. *Freud and Beyond: A History of Modern Psychoanalytic Thought.*

Porges, Stephen W. *The Pocket Guide to Polyvagal Theory: The Transformative Power of Feeling Safe.*

Porter, Roy. *Madness: A Short History.*

———, ed. *The Cambridge Illustrated History of Medicine.*

Schafer, Roy. *A New Language for Psychoanalysis.*

Shay, Jonathan, MD, PhD. *Odysseus in America: Combat Trauma and the Trials of Homecoming.*

Shengold, Leonard, MD. *Soul Murder: The Effects of Childhood Abuse and Deprivation.*

Shorter, Edward, and David Healy. *Shock Therapy: A History of Electroconvulsive Treatment in Mental Illness.*

Sigerist, Henry, ed. *Paracelsus: Four Treatises.*

Solomon, Andrew. *The Noonday Demon: An Atlas of Depression.*

Styron, William. *Darkness Visible: A Memoir of Madness.*

van der Kolk, Bessel, MD. *The Body Keeps the Score: Brain, Mind, and Body in the Healing of Trauma.*

Winnicott, D. W. *The Child and the Family.*

———. *The Child, the Family, and the Outside World*

———. *Playing and Reality.*

———. *Thinking About Children.*